Empowered Recruiting:
The Student-Athlete's College Selection Guide

Julianne Soviero

DEDICATION

This is for everyone out there who has ever had the dream of playing a sport in college. It isn't just luck or pure athletic skill. It is a lot of work, planning, and perseverance. With the help of this book, you can definitely do it!!!

CONTENTS

Julianne Soviero

ACKNOWLEDGMENTS

This book would not have been possible without the thousands of experiences my amazing athletes have afforded me. We have taught each other: guiding them has helped me to understand recruiting at every level. Several of my athletes have even contributed chapters to help the readers to better understand what the recruiting process is like from their perspectives.

Rob Crews and A-Game have also had a huge impact on the creation of this book. Rob knows pretty much everything about networking and college recruiting, and the A-Game program reflects that. Rob is also a great person to talk to when I want to lament the inequities of the college recruiting process.

My husband, Frank, is a terrific editor and my biggest supporter. He is also very fond of saying, "if I had read this book in high school, I would not have had any student loans!" That is probably very true.

Thank you to Vega, particularly Trevor Ellestad, for making the best sports performance products ever. Knowing that I have the encouragement of such innovative and amazing people is invaluable to me.

Finally, I wouldn't know the first thing about the college recruiting process if I hadn't lived through it myself. Playing at a Division I level was something that I had always wanted to do, but it would have been impossible without the help of my amazing parents. My Mom and Dad walked me through the process and supported me every step of the way. They did their research and encouraged me to do mine.

Julianne Soviero

A Must-Read Introduction
By Rob Crews

I was in sunny Florida, sitting in an empty bleacher at a "Softball Showcase." There were people that traveled to this event from all over the country. Parents missed work, players missed school, and hotels were at maximum occupancy. Tons of revenue, resources, and time were being spent: mainly by the player's families.

You might think that this is a rare event, but it's not. There are dozens and dozens of events like this happening all over the country in all different sports, and they are making a ton of money for the people who create them.

I removed myself from a crowded bleacher where a team from the South was playing a team from the Northeast. I needed to check my messages and return some phone calls in private. A woman came over and sat a few rows up. I couldn't help but overhear her phone conversation:

"Yeah, so I am down here in Florida. My granddaughter is playing in some softball tournament for little rich kids. It is supposed to be a college thing and I haven't seen more than 3 schools here. And they just stop the games right in the middle, and there are no winners. What is this?"

She went on and on and I was laughing inside, not only because she was funny: I was laughing because she was right!

In my years of working with the families of baseball and softball players, I have seen the college recruiting process evolve into this monster. Yes, it has become somewhat of a monster: mostly because we have allowed it to become that. The only way to safeguard ourselves from falling victim to the economic and time-depleting woes of the recruiting process is to be as educated as possible. Finding someone that is 100% honest with you is not easy, because the recruiting process has morphed from a sincere platform for youth development into a corporate machine -one that can manipulate good people. The ignorance of eager parents is getting taken advantage of as they pursue their children's dreams. I have seen the best people in the world become the biggest liars and manipulators: all in the name of a dollar. It's like they have forgotten the players. They have forgotten the children. They have forgotten that these are people's hopes and dreams.

So let's break down the three main points of what the woman in the bleachers had deduced:

Point 1 - She referred to this showcase as a softball tournament for "*little rich kids.*"

Yes, the game has gotten pretty expensive. Travel sports have become mostly about money and exclusively for those who can afford to play, even though they might not necessarily be the best players. In softball, for instance, if a team runs a tryout for 200 players, they pick the best players and give them the pricing structure. They will give those players 24 hours to make a decision and then move to the weaker players who may perhaps want to buy themselves a roster spot. Many of the more reputable teams can charge even more money and those teams may have 3 or 4 teams competing in the same age range. Obviously, if you're not on the "main" team, you are treated as a second class citizen and sent to the weaker showcases. Or maybe you are sent to the same showcases and you are playing on the worse geographically located fields -fields that college coaches wouldn't dare drive to. Some teams go so far as to allow weaker athletes to basically pay the fees of another player. Stay with me because it gets better. That same benchwarmer may even show up to a tournament and find a guest player taking her at bats or playing time. Instead of the 14-player roster she thought she signed up for, it has become an 18-player roster. In this scenario, the value of each player's experienced has just decreased.

Point 2 - "It is supposed to be a college thing. I haven't seen more than 3 colleges here."

If you bought a doughnut with no sugar in it or a slice of pizza with no sauce on it, you would be upset. On the other hand, if you get swindled or manipulated by a team or a showcase event, you don't say anything. You never complain. The common thought process is that it could hurt your child's chances of being recruited. Let me help you. The only things that hurt your child's chances of being recruited are being mediocre in talent, having poor scholastic aptitude, or having a poor attitude. The bottom line is that an athlete needs to be good enough and smart enough to earn the attention of college coaches. I am not just referring to being smart in the classroom. Athletes have to be smart enough to educate themselves and their families about the whole recruiting process. I am the founder of a successful college selection and education system that is rooted in those two premises: good enough, and smart enough. We focus on athletic, academic, and personal development. I would never lie to a client about their current capabilities. If they have the work ethic to change, then we can project an upside. If not, then they have probably peaked, and shouldn't be pursuing schools that are beyond their capabilities. Playing endless "showcases" devoid of college coaches are not getting you any closer to your collegiate goals. You need someone who will be honest with you so you can focus on your development

Point 3 - "And they just stop the games right in the middle, and there's no winners. What is this?"

I know you are laughing to yourself. You are laughing about the drop-dead 70 minute games in which your daughters who bat 6th or 7th probably only get 1 or 2 at bats. The tournaments that use this format become less competitive and players focus only on themselves, rarely experiencing how to be a team player. I could go on, but I will leave it right here.

The modern model for showcasing and recruiting seems to revolve around a series of single events. These events are usually college showcases or college camps. In this scenario, the pressure is on because most players feel as though they have to get it done in that particular moment. The truth of the matter is that recruiting and selection is a process: one that involves developing an organic relationship with college coaching staffs over time. It is almost never about one performance or event.

Let's use the prom as an analogy for the current showcasing model. You wouldn't even think about going to such an important social event unless you were properly prepared. This means that you need to have a dress, shoes, accessories, hair and makeup, and you would also need a date. You would have a better chance of having a good time if your date shares your interests and there is mutual trust involved. If there has been no genuine effort to make yourself appealing enough to be invited, and no one has shown any interest, it would be downright dumb to spend a lot of money on expensive prom accessories just to show up and have a miserable time by yourself. Yet so many athletes don't take the time to develop relationships with coaches before a showcase. So many athletes do not understand basic base-running, throwing, fielding and other fundamentals. Yet they show up at the showcase (prom) like, "Look at me! I'm here!

Does anybody see me? Does anybody like me? Does anybody want to recruit me? Does anybody want me to be a part of their program?"

You can see where people end up wasting a lot of time and money. We have all these athletes showing up to these showcases and 3 swings into the first game it becomes painfully obvious that they don't belong. It's the equivalent of a C+ student applying to Harvard. Sadly, this is the climate for college recruiting. It is sad that these players have no one to tell them the truth. They need to know about their true capabilities as an athlete, based on their work ethic or lack thereof. Most travel teams are advising athletes based on what will look good for their website, not what is appropriate for the players. Travel ball coaches often push players towards their "favorite schools": a small network whom the coaches are friends with. Parents are often advising their players based on their own egos, not what is suitable to the child. When are we really looking at what would be best for the child?

The college selection process is no fairy tale. It is hard work and dedication, just like anything else in life. If you are not prepared academically, physically and organizationally, then someone else will be. Don't let people who are trying to make money off of you tell you or your child that you are better than you really are. Be honest with yourself and be dedicated to your pursuits. By reading this book, you have taken the first step to taking control back. Education about the recruiting process is the key to finding the college that is right for you. To be educated is to be empowered. Welcome to Empowered Recruiting.

1 IT'S ABOUT TO GET REAL

First and foremost, accept my apologies. This is an excellent book, but I am sorry that the recruiting process has become so dreadfully complicated that you actually NEED an entire book dedicated to guiding you through the experience. The truth is, college coaches are recruiting athletes who are younger and younger. Consequently, athletes have to be made aware of the recruiting process well before most of them are ready.

I'm not going to lie. It stinks.

Actually, I have many friends who are college coaches, and they don't like it either. It creates problems for them too. For one, some athletes peak very early. They "verbal" (a term we will discuss in detail later) at a very young age and then don't improve. This might just be a matter of physically maturing early on, or perhaps hitting a "mental slump" after achieving a certain level of success. For other young athletes, the primary goal is ONLY to get a scholarship. This is a problem for coaches because once these recruits know that they have earned a scholarship, they stop working and often regress. Meanwhile, other athletes who showed less skill at a younger age have become incredible, but coaches have committed all of the funds they were allotted.

You can see where this would create problems for everyone.

So why do coaches recruit so early to begin with? Essentially, they are afraid that if they don't verbal great athletes early, the next Jennie Finch will go to a rival school. Coaches, just like athletes, are afraid of losing huge opportunities.

But is it really worth it?

The recruitment of 13 year-old athletes is also affecting the atmosphere in travel ball. Kids are now under a lot of pressure from their travel team coaches to start specializing in *only* one sport immediately, so that they can focus on getting recruited. I once had a seventh grader tell me that her travel coach would not allow her to continue to play on the travel team unless she quit *all of* her other sports. This girl was a tremendous three-sport athlete. Oh, and did I mention that she was in SEVENTH GRADE? Most travel coaches are not certified personal trainers or athletic trainers and do not realize that early specialization is pretty much the quickest road to injury. You can't get recruited if you are on the bench due to an injury.

If you had told me ten years ago that college coaches would be recruiting 12 year-olds, I would have laughed and said you had lost your mind. Unfortunately, this is what is actually happening! Early specialization and recruiting is not only a problem in terms of physical burnout, it creates mental burnout as well. As a certified hypnotist and Havening Practitioner, I work with a lot of young athletes for whom the pressure of recruiting is simply too much. Often, we work through it with hypnosis or Havening. But sometimes, it is evident that these pressures affect the athlete in such a terrible way, that I feel it is in the child's best interest to actually quit the sport. This is a very sad situation, but the athletes face so much pressure from coaches, parents, and themselves to perform at their best all of the time. Sometimes, they simply can't handle all of that plus school and social pressures. Many athletes are led to believe that scholarships are much more common than they actually are. Truthfully, only around five percent of all high school athletes earn ANY kind of athletic scholarship (forget about a "full ride"). Many young athletes don't know that fact. Their ignorance in this matter (or perhaps their parent's ignorance) allows them to feel like failures if they don't get some kind of compensation for their athletic efforts.

The other problem with early recruiting is the fact that most young athletes don't yet know exactly what they want to study in college. How many seventh graders do *you* know who are certain of exactly what they want their college experience to be like? I thought so. Yet many eighth graders are making verbal commitments to high-level Division I schools. They get caught up in the glitz and the glamour of being recruited. Then, FIVE YEARS later, when they discover that the school they chose is not actually in line with their values, they have to go through the miserable processing of transferring. We will discuss that a little bit later in the book, but I pray you don't have to go through it. I have been though it multiple times with my athletes, and I would advise you to avoid it by choosing a compatible school the first time around. Transferring as an athlete is complicated, stressful, and full of paperwork.

Do athletes who earn full scholarships really change their minds? Do they really find that they hate a school so much that they can't endure it for four years? Yes. I had one of my athletes (now happily finishing her athletic career at a Division II school) earn a full ride to a big school down south. She was very young when she was recruited. She essentially went to the school because she loved the softball program, but she didn't really know what she wanted academically. When she actually began attending the school and decided on a major, she realized that it was impossible to keep all of the academic commitments required by her major while keeping all of the travel commitments required by her sport. While away at school, she also realized that she missed her family and friends from home and didn't feel accepted in her new environment. This was a huge problem since it took her parents over eight hours of travel time to get to her college. This made her homesick and even a bit panicked. What was essentially her dream school when she was fourteen became a nightmare when she was eighteen.

Many businesses have also capitalized on the fact that athletes are starting the recruiting process younger and younger. Have you noticed that suddenly there are a million "showcases" and "recruiting events" out there? It is usually over two hundred dollars to attend and there are hundreds of athletes there, but maybe only a few coaches. Do the math for a second. How much are the people hosting the showcases making? Compare that against the odds of you getting seen by the coach or coaches that you want to be seen by. Oh, and did I mention you can pay a measly additional $500 dollars to have a terrible skills video done? It's a complete rip off. There are some reputable showcases out there, but most of them are just making tons of money for the people running them and not bringing you any closer to your dream school.

Even if you decide to opt out of bad showcases, you will still be spending a ton of money on the recruiting process by traveling to different campuses, paying to be on an elite travel team, paying to stay in hotels, paying for private coaches, personal trainers, and chiropractors/doctors. The list goes on and on. You might even pay someone to help you find that special school. Here too, you have to be very careful of scams. I have had "recruiters" approach my athletes (after NEVER even seeing them play) and tell the athletes that they can help them get a scholarship. There are a few reputable programs that I think are worth the investment, but the majority of these programs are scams.

If you take all of the money you are putting into getting recruited and invest it conservatively, you can probably pay for college yourself.

There has got the be a better way!

I am proudly an A-Game consultant and I think that it is a great program. I have helped so many athletes find their dream schools, even before I was a part of A-Game. I have really been doing this for over thirteen years. I have definitely noticed that the athletes whom I consult with using the A-Game Initial Consultation do much better in the recruiting process and are much happier in their chosen schools than their peers. The reason for this is simple: we are taking the time to sit down with you and your family and develop a customized plan. We are making sure that everyone is on the same page. Even if that family doesn't decide to make a huge commitment by doing the A-Game Masters Program (and most of them don't), they still have all of the information they need to make a good decision. On the other hand, people who try to pick my brain "for free" never end up getting much out of it. They don't get an opportunity to see the whole picture. These are inevitably the same people that end up scrambling during junior and senior year, somehow shocked that all of the schools they are contacting committed their scholarship funds elsewhere years ago. These are people who don't understand that spending a little money and time initially can save them thousands and thousands of dollars in the long run.

I can't do an A-Game Consultation with everyone, though I firmly believe that every serious athlete needs one. Fortunately, just by reading this book, you should be able to avoid the typical pitfalls that can make the college recruiting process really miserable.

So let's get started, shall we? Use this book in an interactive way. Mark off different pages, highlight different sections, and take notes in the margins. This book is meant to help you determine where you want to go and whether or not that is attainable. I want you to be educated about the process. I want you to be successful. I want you to be among the five percent of athletes that gets that scholarship. You will be shocked to know this, but it isn't just about talent. It is about marketing and exposure. It is about who you know. It is about how you educate and organize yourself throughout the recruiting process. Treat the following pages like a treasure map leading you to your dreams.

2 THE ANATOMY OF YOUR DREAM SCHOOLS

This chapter is very purposely about "dream schools" (emphasis on the plural), because, despite what you might think now, you will be very happy at more than one school. The idea that everyone has one school that she is destined to find like some weird academic soul mate is completely irrational. If you are searching using the right criteria, you should be able to find several schools that fit your academic interests, preference for location, and your atheltic aspirations. It is important to look at several schools because it is possible that you won't get accepted to some. It is also possible that the school you like best is done recruiting for your position and/or year. Finally, several schools pursuing you can allow you to make a better decision financially when it comes time to verbal or sign your National Letter of Intent.

So where to start? It depends on your age. If you are in 7th grade, you can start by looking at schools that might be "a reach" for you but have piqued your interest. These schools might be competing in your sport on television or they might be a long shot for you academically. The younger you are, the higher you can aspire. If you have always wanted to go to UCLA, there is no risk to going to one of their camps or clinics as an 7th grader and requesting a meeting with the coach after. One of my athletes went to a few Texas clinics when she was younger, but seeing her "dream school" really made her realize that college softball was not for her. Here's the thing: that is completely fine. Very few athletes visit their supposed "dream school" and still idolize it afterwards. It is better if you find that out immediately so you can start to really focus on what will actually make you happy.

Now, if you are older (let's say a junior), it might be very impractical to pay a visit to schools that are "a reach." The reason for this is simple: most of the big Division I schools have already verbaled their star athletes at a

11

young age. Currently, in 2016, many of the more recognizable Division I schools are looking at 2020 graduates. Absurd, but true! There are occasionally athletes who "deverbal" (something we will talk about later) from these schools or become academically ineligible. These are pretty much the only cases in which high-profile Division I schools will have funds open up for a high school junior, and it is becoming increasingly rare. As a junior, you have to get realistic pronto. Look at schools that fit the criteria that you will develop in this chapter, even if those schools don't have some of the glitz and glam of the schools you see on television.

The next few pages contain some guidelines to get you thinking about things that will make you happy in a school. You want to consider your academic interests, your athletic interests, geography, demographic, size, and campus look/layout. Much of this research can be done on this fancy new thing called a computer, but some of it really requires that you go to the school. Some of the pictures that you see online aren't even taken on campus, so you really need to check things out for yourself. Consider the following questions:

Academic Interests

- Do they have your intended major and your intended minor? These seem like really obvious questions to ask, but you would be surprised how many athletes search by their sport first. This is something you should NEVER EVER do.
- Can you study both the major you want and the minor you want, or is your schedule inflexible? I orginally wanted to be an English Education major and minor in Fine Arts. When I was down to my last two schools, one of them required that I double major in English and Education in order to obtain my degree. This really convinced me to go to the other school because I didn't have the opportunity to choose even one elective with a required double major. At Manhattan College, I was able to be a Psychology Minor (I changed my mind: it happens) and still take an art class through a program at a sister school. I definitely made the right decision.
- What sort of internship/mentorship programs are available? Many athletes think about the experience of going to school, but they think very little about how that experience will help them to get a job in the real world. This was not something that I actually considered when I was looking at schools, but I advise all my

athletes to do it now. Some schools have a terrific network of alumni in addition to mentoring programs. Some schools have great relationships with specific firms. Find out! Your dream school should help lead you to your dream career.

- What are the alumni who chose your major currently doing? If most of the Physical Education Majors from your school are currently working retail, reconsider.

- What is the average income for graduates ten years after graduation? This may seem silly, but many schools have a terrible return on investment (ROI). Some schools that you might think will automatically get you a job won't do as much for you as you think. There is a great website that will give you more infomration about this: www.payscale.com/college-education-value

- What kind of course load will you have to take? This is a really important question to ask as an athlete. You are going to have times when you are overwhelmed by athletic and academic responsibilites. Knowing exactly how many credits you need to take in order to graduate on time is very important.

- Could you study abroad/do coursework over the summer? I love learning. I wanted to take as many classes as possible, but I also found that taking Italian during Fall Ball was a terrible decision. I didn't understand it at all and I knew I would have to drop it. Fortunately, I was able to do a month abroad over the summer and fulfill my language requirements that way. Not only that, but I learned so much faster living in Italy than I ever could have living in the Bronx. That was a skill that served me very well when I coached in Italy. I was already familarized with the language and culture from an academic experience that I probably couldn't have gotten if I went to another school.

- Is it an academcially competitive school? This might not be important to everyone, but it was very important to me. I like the idea of challenging my mind and I didn't want to go to a school where the professors weren't PHDs. That is a value choice. You might want professionals and adjuncts teaching your classes. You have to decide what is best for you.

- How big are the classes? One of the biggest scams out there is the idea that many of these colleges list something like an 18:1 student to teacher ratio. Here is the thing: they are including graduate students and assistants in that ratio along with the PHDs. The classes are actually over a hundred students. This is where it becomes extremely important to actually sit in on a class. Decide if you are comfortable with the amount of students there, the layout of the classrooms, and the professors themselves. Many schools are now doing a lot of their classes online. I could personally never learn that way, but if you can, you would probably save some money by just attending an online university and learning in the comfort of your home.

Now that you are familiar with some academic criteria, list five (or more) schools you are interested in for academic reasons:

1.

2.

3.

4.

5.

Athletic Interests

- What are the facilities like? Though this wasn't really a major factor for me when I was researching schools, I know that it is very important to some athletes. Notice what the fields/courts are like. Are they well-maintained? Do you have to share your field with another sport? What kind of resources do you have available to you as far as gym equiptment, prehab/rehab facilities, locker rooms and practice facilities?
- Do athletes get special perks or privileges? At most schools, athletes get to register for classes first to accommodate their practice and travel schedules, but this isn't the case at every school.
- Do athletes get more academic support? Most Division I schools require study hall for freshman. I think this is a wonderful idea, and it will help you to learn to manage your time as a young athlete. Many of my athletes are afraid of going Division I because they feel that the academic commitment will be too much when coupled with sports. Ironically, many of them have not done any research regarding the support Division I schools provide their athletes. If you struggle in a particular subject, many (but not all) Division I programs will actually get you a tutor for that subject. This happens in other Divisions as well, but since Division I schools generally have more money and resources, they can usually provide a bit

more assistance. Division I and academic success are definitely both attainable. You just have to make sure that your major is compatible with your sport at a Division I level. Some majors just aren't. For example, majoring in music usually involves heavy band requirements. Other majors might involve a lot of lab time and/or interning. These are things that might make playing a sport and going to school nearly impossible. If you think that your intended major might have similar requirements, do some research. Don't use your potential coach as your only source of information. You need to talk to students who have currently accepted all of the responsibilities required of your intended major. Ask them about their time commitments and consider whether or not those time commitments will be feasible with your sport's schedule. You don't want to discover that it will never work AFTER you have signed your Letter of Intent.

- Can you see yourself playing for this coach? Let's face it, we all have a particular type of coach for whom we play our best. It is hard to tell in just a few interactions whether or not a college coach will be a good match for you, but DO YOUR HOMEWORK. Talk to both current and former players. Ask them questions about coaching style and coach/player interactions. I have heard some horror stories about how coaches have treated players. On the positive side of that, many athletes who have been through that want to save others from the same experience and are quick to share their insights. I knew going into college that my coach was well-meaning and nice, but she wasn't my "dream coach." I chose my school anyway because of the academics and location. If I had gone to a school strictly for the coach I wanted (which would have been Bill Edwards of Hofstra), I don't think I would have had the same great academic experience. I definitely made the right decision for me. There are other factors that you will want to consider when you are meeting prospective coaches. You definitely want to know how long that coach has been at that school. You also want to know if that coach has another job at the school. Why? Many coaching positions are low-paying and coaches have to move on if they have another offer. If your prospective coach is otherwise employed by the school, there is a better chance that he or she will stick around. You don't EVER want to choose a school only for the coach, but you also don't want to think you have made a reasonable decision about a program only to find out that the coach you thought you would have for four years was replaced by a lunatic. It happens, so do some research.

- Is the program for your sport at a level of play that you can handle? Many athletes are very confused about what level they should be looking to play at. I have seen some athletes who would barely make a Division III team claiming that they want to go Division I. Someone needs to send them a wakeup call! On the other hand, one of my very talented athletes told me a few months ago that she was looking at a Division III school that was a bad program coupled with bad academics. I told her there was no way I would let her go there and forced her to start looking elsewhere. Sure enough, she just got a few offers from some very good Division II schools and she happily signed with one of them. Many athletes really have no idea where they belong. You need someone whom you trust to really help you out here. You might be very talented, but lazier than a sloth. If this is the case, Division I is definitely out and Division II is probably out as well. Talk to someone who knows your skill level, personality, and work ethic. Don't just listen to that "recruiter" who will tell you whatever you want to hear.

- What kind of resources does the athletic program offer? Some schools provide athletic trainers, personal trainers, and coaches who work specifically with your position. Although many athletes might choose a program because they like an assistant coach or trainer, this is not in any way advisable. These coaches are typically paid very little and are often gone within a year or two. It's nice to look at the different people you will have at your disposal, but don't base your decision on any one person.

- What is the team atmosphere like? Some teams can be very segmented and filled with drama. Some teams are very hardworking. Some try to get away with as little work as possible. My college team had a good mix of girls and almost everyone got along. I had visited other schools where I felt a lot of division among different members of the team even during a visit! Imagine what that would be like over four years. Yuck. Also, if you want nothing more than to play your sport and excel at it, make sure you are not looking at teams where the work ethic is lackluster. That will make you miserable. Even Divison I athletes often like to drink and party. In some schools, this is really prevalent, and in others it is not. Try to figure it out, especially on your official visit. On one of my official visits, the girl I was staying with offered me drugs. That pretty much knocked the school off of my list for good. I didn't want to be in any kind of enviroment like that. Many of the athletes whom I have helped to transfer do so because

16

there was way too much drinking/promiscuity/partying on the team. Look for red flags on your visits. The team will be your make-shift family for four years. They have to be people who share similar values with you. You may also have to consider the gay/straight issue here. This didn't make a difference to me because I was comfortable either way, but if you are a lesbian and you find yourself on a team where the coach (or the players) are unaccepting of your lifestyle, you will be very unhappy. Conversely, if you are straight and you are on a team where you are the only straight guy or girl, that could be an uncomfortable situation. No one is judging you: this is your decision. YOU will have to be comfortable with what you choose for four years. Though this was not a factor at all for me in school selection since I have always had many close friends in the LBGT community, I could understand where this could be a very important issue for some people. This is probably not something you would ask the coach about. Use your intuition and deductive reasoning skills.

- Do athletes have to live on campus? If you were planning on living at home during college, this is something you want to ask about. Some coaches require that their athletes dorm because of early morning workouts, travel schedules and so on. Get all the information, especially if you aren't planning on living on campus.

Now that you know some criteria that will help you look for the right athletic fit, list five (or more) schools that you would be intersted in for athletic reasons:

1.

2.

3.

4.

5.

Geography/Location

- How far are you from home? A plane ride isn't always a bad thing, but there are some places that are inherently difficult to get to. For example, I visited Stanford, which is essentially in the middle of three major airports. You will have no trouble getting there. Virginia Tech, on the other hand, is not particularly close to many airports and can be a long drive from many areas. If you live in NY, you might think Stanford is insanely far, but it is convenient to get to. Virginia Tech looks closer on paper, but it is about a nine hour drive and it takes a similar amount of time to get there by air.

- What is the climate like? I originally wanted to go south because I despise the cold. I have some athletes who love the cold and want to go up north. Some people think they want to live in Florida until they deal with the oppressive humidity on a daily basis. My desire to go south was eventually supplanted by my desire to be near the culture and art of NYC, but don't completely ignore your climate preferences.

- Do you like urban or rural? The more I considered it, rural was just really not a good option for me. I love museums, good restaurants, and lots of diversity. Rural areas don't always offer these luxuries. If you would like something a little more rural (maybe you want a school where the college football game is the most exciting thing happening on a Saturday night), you might want a little bit of a bigger school. Those can really act like their own cities in many ways.

- Can you walk to a surrounding area or take a subway there? This is an important consideration since some schools do not allow cars on campus. Mass transit is not always available in rural areas.

- Would you feel comfortable on campus in this area? Does it seem safe? I have had many athletes decide against certain schools because of the perceived safety of surrounding areas.

List five or more schools that you are interested in for location:

1.

2.

3.

4.

5.

Size/Demographic

- Is there enough diversity among the student body? This could be cultural diversity or fiscal diversity. My high school had about 500 kids who were exactly the same in every way: I hated it. I wanted something totally different in college. I was really happy to be around people in college who came from all different backgrounds. It really broadened my horizons and let me be myself.

- Are there activities to do other than sports? Do you want a school that is run by jocks? Maybe you do. Far be it from me to judge. But if your sport is not your only interest, check to see if volunteer programs are available or clubs that may be of interest to you. This is a great way to meet people outside of your sport. Though I loved playing sports in college, one of my best experiences was on a service trip to Puerto Rico. Go figure! That wasn't even something I would have been interested in as a high school student, but Manhattan's Lasallian tradition inspired me to get more involved.

- Do many students go home on weekends? This is extremely important. I was at a school where I COULD go home on the weekend if I needed/wanted to, but I rarely did. Hello, NYC, aka the best place to spend the weekend ever! I wasn't going anywhere. Other schools I looked at cleared out on weekends. That was something I wanted to avoid.

- How many students go to the school and what are the class sizes like? Do they include graduate students when they are quoting student to teacher ratios?

List 5 (or more) schools that you are interested in based on demographics.

1.

2.

3.

4.

5.

Campus

- Aesthetics: What does it look like? Is it your taste/style? Some people love a contemporary look while others enjoy a more classic appearance. You should enjoy the way the campus looks. You should like spending time at the mall (not a shopping mall) on nice days.
- How spread out is the campus? Would you need a bike or a car to get from one class to another? This is a really important consideration, especially if you aren't allowed to have a car on campus or storing a bike might be difficult.
- Is the campus in the middle of a city (where dorming might be difficult and/or expensive) or is it very rural (where it's possible that many students may go home over the weekend)?
- Are they expanding the campus? Remember, you will be there for four years, and if you like the idea of a small school, but the school is designed to get bigger, that is a factor that you want to consider.
- Is there parking on campus and does it matter? It does matter if you are going to be student teaching or interning while you are taking classes. Is the parking free? If you have to pay a lot to park your car on campus, that can increase your tuition bill significantly.
- What are the dorms like? I didn't think I could possibly deal with a shower down the hallway. I was just way too shy for all of that. I didn't need anything high tech, I just wanted to avoid walking down the hall in my bathrobe. What kind of dorm situation are you most comfortable in? What are the dorms like for upperclassman?

- Does the campus reflect your values and have options for the type of diet you have? There are many schools that now offer organic and vegan options. Some schools even have their own compost or their own gardens. If I was looking for a school now, this would be a very high priority for me. Schools accommodate a lot of people and so they need to be aware of their impact on the environment. This may not be something that you care about (although you should!), but I could never go to a school that was feeding everyone processed food and throwing out all of the leftovers. Recycling on campus is another thing that would be crucial for me.

List 5 (or more) schools you would be interested in based on the campus

1.

2.

3.

4.

5.

You should now have a list of several schools that you are interested in. You might find that a few of the schools repeat themselves. Congratulations! You are well on your way to finding your *actual* dream school(s). If you have not already visited these campuses, get going! If you haven't seen ANY campuses yet, I strongly recommend that you look at as many as possible when you are traveling to play sports. Do this even if the school is not of interest to you intitially. The more you see, the more you will realize what you do and don't like. I had already seen so many campuses by the time I was in 9th grade. This was a huge advantage! It can also be a lot of fun and a great way to spend quality time with your parents.

It is now time to begin creating a filing cabinet, Excel spreadsheet, or a computer file. Fill these files with impressions, ideas, prices, contacts with coaches, and any other information pertinent to your school search. You really need to be organized here! We will discuss more about contacting coaches in future chapters, but you are going to need to customize your letters and keep track of contacts. You can't do that properly if everything is disorganized. If organization is not your strongest attribute, get a parent or older sibling to help you. You will be glad you did it!

Chapter Review

1. Think about the criteria that are most important for you when looking for a school: consider academic needs, the look and layout of different campuses, school demographics, geography, and the athletic program.
2. Using these criteria, either do an internet search, sit down with your guidance counselor, or schedule an A-Game consultation.
3. Know what it is that you value and make sure that any potential schools align with those values.
4. Talk to current and former students at the school, particularly the student-athletes.
5. Find a way to get organized. If you prefer paper, get a filing cabinet and use it exclusively for information from prospective schools and coaches. Tech savvy athletes can use Excel or create digital files.

3 KNOW ALL OF YOUR OPTIONS

There are a lot of things you need to know about the different divisions in college sports. You are probably only familiar with the NCAA at this point. The NCAA is a governing body. Some of your prospective schools may choose to be members of the NCAA, but other schools may make a different choice. I like to describe it this way to my A-Game consultations: picture the governing organizations in college sports like different countries. NCAA is kind of like America: we all know about it, and sometimes we act like it is the only game in town. It is possible, however, that you don't meet the criteria necessary to be a part of the NCAA or you simply don't agree with their philosophies. You are free to go someplace else! Just like there are different laws in different countries, the different governing bodies in college sports have different rules and criteria. What follows is the break down of NCAA, Ivy, NAIA and NJCAA. Most of you will probably play in the NCAA, but that is not your only option. If you are not a strong student, you might want to look into the NJCAA exclusively since you might not meet NCAA academic standards.

NCAA

This is the organization that most of you are familiar with. All of the college championships that you see on television are NCAA. You can find out almost everything you need to know about the NCAA at www.ncaa.org. There are also several other resources on that website for your college recruiting journey. Though other organizations also have different divisions, when most people refer to Divisons I, II, and III, they are referring to NCAA schools. Here is a brief look at what the different NCAA Divisions are like:

- **Division I** – Less than 5% of all athletes go Division I. This is a huge commitment. You must understand that you will be living and breathing your sport for four years. If you are not up for that, start looking someplace else. Prior to going to Division I, you must not only be committed, but should already have experience on a high profile, very competitive team. You should also want to play and excel at your sport *more than you want to do anything else.* You must be the best in your league, team, and state. You must know that if you intend to "walk on" in Division I, you will very likely be playing left bench. Financially, most DI schools have 12 full scholarships or less to split over the entire team. That's only 2-4 per year. Now you understand why coaches have started recruiting so young. Good coaches plan for the years ahead. There are definitely Division I schools that play at a much higher caliber than others. The teams you see in the College World Series are the highest level Division I in the country. Some Division I schools are in their first year after converting from Division III. These schools, though technically Division I, are definitely not as competitive. There can be a major difference from one program to the next, so it is important to do your homework. There are 335 Division I Softball Schools in the US.

- **Division Two** – In this division there are tremendous variations in competitiveness and commitment. Some have amazing and very competitive programs that can beat Division I schools. Other programs would get killed by a good D III school. You therefore have to do your homework on each DII school you are interested in. Check out their records and the coach's philosophy. Still not sure? Go to a clinic. If it is run well and emphasizes discipline, then they are competitive and you will probably live and breathe your sport there. If it is disorganized or otherwise poorly run, you can probably bet that they are not very competitive. The NCAA puts a lot more restrictions on how much practice time you can engage in at the Division II level, so most athletes assume that it is "easier." That is not necessarily the case at all. If you are interested in the the perspective of someone who has transferred from Division I to Division II, skip right to Chapter 12. Division II only has about 7 full scholarships to split among its team

24

members. This means only about 1-3 per year. There are 269 Divison II Softball Schools in the US.

- **Division Three** – There is once again a tremendous degree of variability when it comes to the level of competitiveness here. Ask current and former players about their schedules when you are looking at Division III schools. Though the NCAA does put the most restrictions on practice time for Division III, you might still have lots of "optional" practices. This depends largely on your coach. No money is EVER given for athletic scholarships in Division III, but I have somehow never had a talented pitcher go to a Division III school without getting some substantial academic help (even if her SATS didn't set her up for that kind of scholarship). Hmmmmm. There are 408 Division III Softball schools.

Ivy Schools

These are technically NCAA schools, but they deserve their own paragraph, since they have some unique features. Ivy Schools are Division I Schools with rigorous academic standards. Ivy Schools are obviously not something that you should consider unless you have outstanding grades and excellent standardized test scores. One other reason you might NOT want to consider them at all, however, is that fact that they DO NOT provide ANY athletic scholarships. This is a quote directly from the Ivy League website (go to www.ivyleaguesports.com for more information): "Ivy League schools provide financial aid to students, including athletes, only on the basis of financial need as determined by each institution's financial aid office. There are no academic or athletic scholarships in the Ivy League." The Ivy schools are Brown University, Columbia University, Cornell University, Dartmouth College, Harvard University, University of Pennsylvania, Princeton University and Yale University.

NAIA

These are typically small schools that recruit like big schools. They have varying amounts of money to give from school to school. They are NOT part of the NCAA. There are 209 NAIA schools. There are very few recruiting restricitons. You will discover in later chapters that, in the NCAA, there are very specific guidelines on when coaches can and cannot make contact with you. In the NAIA, you can talk to a college coach at almost any time. For more information, visit www.naia.org.

NJCAA

The NJCAA is comprised of Junior Colleges or two-year schools. Every athlete on an NJCAA Division I team is awarded a full scholarship. NJCAA is very competitive athletically, but not very competitive academically. They belong to the NCAA. NJCAA is a good choice if you aren't sure what you want to do academically or you don't have good grades: www.njcaa.org. The only disadvantage is that you have to go through the entire recruiting process again when you transfer to a four-year school. You would also have to make sure that your credits transfer. NJCAA also has Divsions: Division I (155 schools), Division II (135 schools) and Division III (68 schools).

Hopefully, this chapter helped you to understand ALL of your options. This will help you to avoid wasting time contacting schools that would not be a good fit for you. In the next chapter, we will discuss some NCAA academic standards, since they have just recently changed. This means that if you are not strong academically, you might not even be elligible to compete in the NCAA. If you are young enough and your grades aren't what they need to be, there is still time to change, but get on it now!

Chapter Review

1. The NCAA is divided into Divisions I, II, and II.
2. Divison I has the most money for athletic scholarships, Division II has somewhat less, and Division III is not allowed to give ANY athletic scholarships.
3. Ivy Schools are highly competitive academically. Though they are Division I and part of the NCAA, they do not give any athletic scholarships.
4. The NAIA is NOT part of the NCAA and they can recruit with very few restrictions.
5. The NJCAA is comprised of Junior Colleges that offer a lot of money, but are only two-year schools.

4 MAKE SURE YOU ARE ELIGIBLE

Before we get too crazy about contacting coaches, going to showcases, and going to clinics, we need to make sure that you are eligible. I have only ever once made the mistake of assuming that an athlete was in good academic standing. She did everything right with her showcases, clinics, video, and coaching contacts. I couldn't figure out why she wasn't getting recruited. As it turned out, she grudgingly confessed her abysmal GPA and everything became clear. I will never forget the look on her face when she said, "I just didn't think academics mattered that much." I think that many athletes are under the impression that academics *don't* matter that much. Now academics matter more than ever before, since every student-athlete graduating in 2016 or later will be held to higher academic standards than those who came before them. They will need a minimum GPA of 2.3 or higher to compete at a Division I level (it used to be 2.0). From my standpoint, this is a very good thing, but I do realize that many people are not aware of this change (sometimes even people in guidance departments!) and so it is up to you to be vigilant and make sure you meet all of the requirements necessary to allow you to compete in the NCAA. Fortunately, this chapter is designed to help you do exactly that.

For Division I, you must have a minimum GPA of 2.3 in your Core Academic courses if you graduate in 2016 or later. The NCAA previously only required a 2.0, so make sure that you adjust accordingly if necessary. In case you are wondering what a "Core" Academic Courses is, "Core Courses" include ONLY Math, English, Social Sciences (like History or Economics) and Science. This is unfortunate for those of you who do not excel in your core courses but are doing great in things like art or autobody. Guess what? Those don't count. If you are struggling academically, you need to sit down with your guidance counselor ASAP and determinse what your GPA is for your CORE COURSES ONLY! You also need to establish a game plan for bringing those grades up. Hit the books, and if you have trouble with comprehension, go for extra help or get a tutor.

I personally encourage my athletes to work hard to be way above the minimum academic requirements since that opens up several more opportunities for scholarships. Believe me, if you have a 4.0 and good SAT scores, a coach who is interested in you will be able to do a lot for you. Plus, if a coach has already recruited for your position and year, but you have an academic scholarship to the school, you can still play for the team but not have to worry about whether or not any money opens up on the athletic side. You have so much more flexibility.

Of course, academic requirements vary greatly for different colleges. I have some very strong high school students with 2000 plus SAT scores who are concerned that their scores aren't high enough for the schools they aspire to attend. Those are pretty unique circumstances, but there are some requirements that are universal:

- You have to complete 16 core courses for eligibility
- 10 of those core courses must be completed by senior year. Make sure that you look at your high school's list of NCAA courses on the NCAA Eligibility Website: www.eligibilitycenter.org. Only the courses that appear on your school's list of NCAA courses will count towards the calculation of your core GPA.
- In Division I, a sliding scale is used to determine your minimum SAT and ACT scores. This will allow you to understand the score(s) you will need to earn in order to compete. Essentially, if you have a very high GPA, your standardized test scores do not need to be as high. Conversely, a lower GPA requires that you generate much higher standardized test scores (see www.NCAA.org for the scale).
- In Divison II, a minimum SAT score of 820 is required. A minimum ACT score of 68 is required in order to compete. A minimum core GPA of 2.0 is required.
- Beginning August 1, 2016, it will be possible for a Division I college-bound student-athlete to still receive athletic aid and the ability to practice with the team if he or she fails to meet the 10 course requirement. That individual would not be able to compete in games, though. I would strongly recommend avoiding this route if at all possible.

If you haven't had any exposure to standardized tests yet, I recommend that you get as much exposure as possible as early as possible. Even students with strong GPAs can do poorly on the standardized tests. This happens because the format, the length of time required to complete the tests, and the pressure can be a little daunting. You must acclimate (look this word up if you don't know it, it might be on your SATs) to these circumstances in order to excel. The more you practice using these testing formats, the better you will be at taking these tests. You can also take both the SAT and ACT several times for grade improvement. Many of my athletes do exactly that.

I strongly recommend that you take both the SAT and the ACT, since you might do very well on one and not the other. The major difference between the SAT and ACT is that the ACT is achievement test whereas the SAT is an aptitude test. This means that the ACT measures what you have already learned in school while the SAT tests your reasoning, verbal abilities, and test-taking abilities. Here are some other things that you should know about these two tests:

- The ACT has up to 5 components: English, Mathematics, Reading, Science, and an optional Writing Test.
- The SAT has only 3 components: Critical Reasoning, Mathematics, and a required Writing Test.
- The College Board introduced a new version of the SAT in 2005, with a mandatory writing test. As I am writing this, the SAT is changing once again. Do your best to become familiarized with the new format.
- The ACT continues to offer its well-established test, plus an optional writing test. The ACT Writing Test is typically only taken if it is required by the college(s) you're applying to.
- The SAT has a correction for guessing. That means that you are penalized more for wrong answers than you are for leaving a question

blank. The ACT is scored based on the number of correct answers with no penalty for guessing.

- The ACT has an Interest Inventory that allows students to evaluate their interests in various career options.
- The SAT score used for NCAA purposes includes only the critical Reading and Math sections. The Writing section of the SAT is not used.
- The ACT score used for NCAA purposes is a sum of the following four sections: English, Mathematics, Reading and Science.
- When you register for the SAT or ACT, use the NCAA Eligibility Center code of 9999 to ensure all SAT and ACT scores are reported directly to the NCAA Eligibility Center from the testing agency.

This brings us to Clearinghouse or NCAA Eligibility. You MUST complete the Eligibility requirements in order to compete at a Division I or Division II level as a freshman. Clearinghouse evaluates your academic records to see if you are eligible to participate in Division I or II College Sports as a freshman. Here are some other details:

-You can only register AFTER your junior year
-Go online to www.eligibilitycenter.org and complete the Student Release Form online

When I do an A-Game Consultation, I sometimes spend a lot of time going into greater depth about SAT, ACT, Core Courses, and GPA. Unfortunately, the first time that many people even hear about eligibility requirements is when they sit down for an A-Game Consultation. If you wait until you are a junior to do that and there is no way you can finish the 10 core courses required of you before your senior year, you're screwed. Therefore, I strongly suggest that you sit down with an A-Game Consultant as either an eighth grader, freshman, or sophomore, and go over all of this material in depth. That way, it is customized to your current academic position. After your A-Game Consultation, make an appointment with your guidance counselor. You should go over all of that information with her and make sure that everyone is on the same page. Continue to follow up with your guidance counselor to make sure you are staying on the right track. Your guidance counselor is also extremely important for getting transcripts and other information out to schools. You therefore need to develop a good rapport with her. You don't want to be on the verge of signing your Letter of Intent with your dream school and then run into snags in the guidance department. Use all of the resources at your disposal and make sure you are up-to-date on everything!

Chapter Review and To-Do List

1. Know the difference between "core courses" and other courses. If you are not sure, check with your guidance counselor or www.eligibilitycenter.org.
2. You need a 2.3 minimum GPA to compete at a Divison I level, and a 2.0 to compete at a Divison II level. This GPA includes Core Courses ONLY.
3. You need 16 core courses by the time you graduate, 10 of which must be completed by your senior year.
4. Schedule some time to sit down with your guidance counselor and A-Game consultant
5. Begin getting used to the different formats used in the SAT and ACT as early as possible.
6. Get academic help in any areas where you are struggling. Don't wait: it could destroy your chances of playing in college.

Julianne Soviero

5 FIVE SECRETS TO CONTACTING COACHES

This chapter is basically about creating your own marketing campaign. I am sorry to be the one to tell you this, but no matter how good you are, schools are not going to come knocking on your doorstep. You have to go out there and make sure that they are aware of your athletic prowess, your stunning academics, and your great attitude. There are several different ways to do this, but, in the end, it is really about building relationships. Rob Crews, the creator of the A-Game program, encourages his clients to think of it like dating.

Yes, it is actually exactly like dating.

Have you noticed how one boy always gets the interest of every girl even though there are definitely boys out there who are smarter, funnier, or even more attractive? The fact that many girls are interested in one boy is a major selling point for him. He becomes a topic of conversation in many social circles for this reason. He suddenly has tons of dating options. Meanwhile, no one is paying attention to his smarter, funnier peers.

I don't think there could be a more perfect analogy for recruiting. Work to develop your skills and attitude. Make yourself more attractive for prospective coaches. Start early and expose yourself to the different coaches and programs that you can see yourself "courting." Once you take these steps, you will find that a curious thing happens: many coaches begin to recognize you. Some of the coaches giving you attention will be from schools you have never even heard of before.

Why does this happen?

You need to realize that coaches have their own social circles. I wasn't quite aware of the extent to which this was true until I consulted for a college. Coaches talk to each other at conventions, in between games, and at social gatherings. If you have created a stir among a few coaches, suddenly everyone wants to recruit you. I had one athlete who was being very heavily recruited by a school that just wouldn't work out for her academically. The coach was wonderful and knew that she was a Division I hurler. He told one of his peers about her. This was what ultimately led to her getting a nearly full ride (which, no matter what you might hear, is extremely rare). Another athlete of mine had done some trips to Alabama, Michigan, UPenn and some other very big schools. She was creating quite a buzz by meeting with all of these coaches. By the time she was ready to sign her Letter of Intent to a major Division I school, she had many other top-ranked colleges pursuing her.

Of course, something like this could work against you. If you have a terrible attitude and you show a potential coach that attitude because you don't care about that school, you might be surprised to find that other coaches are suddenly avoiding you like the plague. Additionally, I have found that there are some coaches that are very highly respected among other coaches, and have a great deal of influence. You will mostly be able to tell who these coaches are by doing a little homework. They are usually coaches who are speaking at events that focus on their sport. They are the ones whom other coaches seem to flock to for advice and companionship. If you make a good impression on one of these influencers, you will create an invaluable network without even realizing it. In softball, they are really easy to spot. It is sort of like trying to pick out an alpha wolf. If you even get the time of day from one of these coaches, go out of the way to be courteous, hardworking, and respectful. One of my athletes related a story about how a college coach had come to one of their travel practices in very hot weather. An athlete on the team ran up to the coach and asked her if she would like some water. Now this is just a decent, respectful thing to do, but it is very helpful in establishing rapport. This gave the coach a good sense of who that athlete was. It made the athlete really stand out from everyone else.

Conversely, there are some coaches that really don't get along with other coaches. If you are trying to be wary of this, look for coaches who can't seem to keep assistants for very long or those who don't seem to have a good rapport with their peers. I can think of a few college coaches who have destroyed relationships with travel teams, instructors, and even other coaches over pretty much nothing. These are the types whom you should respect and listen to, but ultimately, if this is not someone you trust, you don't want them ruining other potential relationships. There are going to be lots of other opportunities for you. If you go back to the dating analogy, consider how dating someone who is beneath you makes other suitors think there is something wrong with you. Dating the class stud makes everyone think that you must be great in a way that they were never able to see. Same. Exact. Thing.

In what other ways is recruiting like dating? In the same way that you wouldn't ask someone to marry you the first time you have contact with one another (we hope) or on your first date, you cannot ask a coach or school to commit to you the first time you connect. That's just nuts. Coaches are very put off by behavior like that. You have to foster a long relationship built on trust and mutual goals. Here are some ways to connect once you know what schools you are interested in:

- ❖ Camps/clinics
- ❖ Snail mail or email
- ❖ Phone calls
- ❖ Ask a travel coach, A-Game Consultant or personal coach (like a pitching or hitting instructor) to introduce you
- ❖ Take lessons from, or connect with, one of the school's consultants

Connection Method I: Camps/Clinics

Notice that I did not write "showcases" when I mention the ways you can connect with schools you are interested in. Many years ago, showcases were a useful tool for athletes who wanted to get some exposure. Athletes were able to attract interest during showcases and were therefore able to connect with schools that they might not have found otherwise. Unfortunately, now *everything* is being called a "showcase" because the organizers realized how much money that title was generating. If you go to a clinic or camp run by a school that you like, you will DEFINITELY be seen by that school. The odds of that happening at a showcase are really not very good at all. The schools you like might not even be at that showcase, and, even if they are, what are the odds of them getting to look at you in a game you are playing in? If you go to the clinic for a school you are interested in, and the coaches like what they see, they will ask for your travel ball schedule and then you can be sure that they will get to watch you perform.

Also, don't avoid clinics because you don't think you are fast enough or good enough yet. Coaches understand that you will continue to work and improve. Stop procrastinating. So many athletes miss opportunities because they are waiting until they get better. The great thing about clinics is that they are desgined to help you get better! If a coach sees you throwing 50 as an eighth grader at one of her clinics, and then you are throwing 57 the next year as a freshman, trust me, the improvement will speak volumes for you. Also, even Division I does occasionally recruit "slower" pitchers, because smart coaches are realizing that if all their pitchers throw the same speed, opposing batters won't have a hard time adjusting from one pitcher to the other.

Remember that list of schools you compiled a few chapters back? That's right, the one listing all of the schools that you might be interested in. Look on the website for that school's team and see if they are hosting any camps or clinics. If you are able to go to a camp or clinic hosted at the school there are several benefits to that:

- You get to see the campus. You can potentially even set up a tour with the coach or with one of the players after the clinic.
- You get an inside look at their coaching methods. You can also get some ideas about what the players are like and what the athletic facilities are like.
- You get facetime with the coaches without violating any NCAA regulations.
- You have a reason to contact the coach via phone, email, or snail mail expressing your gratitude because you learned so much etc. etc. Don't be a kiss-ass, but you know what I mean.

When you are searching for college clinics that might be good for you, I recommend trying to attend fall and winter clinics, since the clinics at the end of the season can sometimes interfere with your testing schedule. Definitely look into ALL clinics, but you don't want to have a million tests on your mind in addition to the pressure of performing your best. If there are no clinics listed on the website of a school you are interested in, email the coach and request that she please send you information as soon as a clinic is scheduled.

What most people don't realize is that coaches get hundreds of emails a day. It is absurd. They can't possibly read all of those. If they have already seen you, they are much more likely to respond to you. If you go back to Rob's dating analogy, if you want to get the attention of someone you have a romantic interest in, you probably want to go where you know they will be. You can't just wait in the shadows hoping they will notice you.

Connection Method II: Email or Snail Mail

This brings us to contacting coaches via email or snail mail. One surefire way to get a coach to *never ever* respond to you is by sending out the same letter to everyone. My friends who are college coaches delete these immediately. One of the most important things you can do in your correspondence with coaches is to let them know that you have taken the time to address the letter to them personally. For example, if you are writing them a letter during their season, you might mention how excited you were to see that they just beat a huge rival or made playoffs. Maybe you want to mention how the school itself was just ranked very well academically. Maybe you want to mention that you recently visited the campus and liked how eco-friendly it was. Any of these are good segues for a well-written letter. You will want to follow up your personalized comments about the school with your projected academic interests (to show that you did your research and the school has your major) and the year you will be graduating. You will want to include some of your accomplishments and also a schedule of your upcoming games, so the coach can easily come to see you play. Some players also include a profile or letter of recommendation, but these aren't absolutely necessary initially. Coaches are pretty much never ever going to go to one of your high school games, so make it easier for them by participating in some big travel tournaments where they are likely to be recruiting anyway. Here is an example of a letter I would send out to a coach:

Julianne Soviero
1899 Lakeland Avenue
Ronkonkoma, NY 11779
Email: juliannesoviero@gmail.com
Home: (631) 737-0196
Cell: (555) 555-5555

Dear Coach Edwards,

Congratulations on your recent win against UCLA! I was extremely excited to see Hofstra beat such a highly ranked school and advance in the playoffs. I have been following Hofstra for many years and am currently a sophomore (2018 graduation year) at Ward Melville High School in Setauket, New York. Hofstra has my intended major in Education in addition to a very competitive softball program. I would love to schedule an unofficial visit with you.

I am a pitcher and have been playing on Varsity since I was an eighth grader. I boasted a .89 ERA last year and was an All-County selection. I play for Team Long Island Travel Team. We will be playing several highly-regarded showcases this year. Here is the link to my schedule (insert link here). I am also attaching a list of academic accomplishments in addition to my profile page. You can contact any of my coaches. I have included their contact information at the bottom of this email.

I hope that you have an opportunity to attend one of the showcases or tournaments that I will be competing in this summer. I do plan on attending your fall clinic. Please feel free to contact either my coaches or I regarding any additional information. I look forward to meeting with you and discussing your program.

Sincerely,
Julianne Soviero

Varsity coach name and contact info
Travel coach name and contact info
Pitching/hitting/specialty coach contact info

Though I haven't often been sought out by college coaches regarding possible recruits, it's always wise to include contact information for your private instructors, travel team, and high school team. A coach who knows you have a good rapport with your current coaches will be reassured. Obviously, don't include contact information for anyone who would be unhappy speaking with potential recruiters about you. This is where I think it is an advantage to have a long-term specialty instructor or an A-Game consultant. Those professionals, along with your travel team staff, can act as liaisons between you and interested college coaches. This is important because, in most sports, the latter can't talk to you until the summer after your junior year. Truthfully, most really good athletes have already verbally committed by that time. You really need someone who is willing to enthusiastically go out of their way to consistently communicate on your behalf. This is essentially why the A-Game Masters Program exists.

I would also strongly recommend emailing/mailing the assistant coach, since they are sometimes the first ones to "scout" an athlete (though not always, it depends on the school). Realize that coaches are incredibly busy and won't always get back to you right away. Persistance is key. If you don't get a response, wait a little while and then follow-up with a relevant letter or phone call. If a coach does respond, he or she might say something like, "I can't speak with you because of your age." This is not a bad response to get from a coach! He or she might also request that you fill out something like a survey. Do it as soon as possible. You want the coaches knowing that you are prompt and responsible. Even if you aren't sure if you are interested in the school, send it anyway. It is good practice. If the coach thinks you might be a potential recruit, he or she may also ask for a video. Traditionally, athletes waited until the summer before their senior year to do a video. Now I would suggest doing it *much* sooner. Making a good video takes a lot of pressure off of you. You can always do another one later if you feel that you have improved dramatically.

What about snail mail, you might wonder? One of my athletes got some great results sending customized letters via snail mail because it was such a novelty. She is currently on a full ride to a Division I school. If you would like to do something like that, I would suggest including your letter of introduction (like the letter on the previous page), your profile page, and your upcoming travel schedule.

We will discuss follow-up letters and emails in a minute, but many of you have probably never heard of a profile page before. It is also sometimes referred to as a "player profile." This is an important part of your marketing campaign.

A profile page is usually ONE very well-designed page that includes all of your pertinent information, plus your picture IN YOUR **CURRENT** TRAVEL BALL UNIFORM. Do not make it difficult or confusing for these very busy coaches! Make it so that the picture is consistent with what they will see when they are looking for you on the field. You are not looking for a modeling contract here. If you have changed travel teams, get a current picture. You should include the following in your profile page:

1. Contact information for anyone whom your prospective coach would want to contact. Make it easy for them. They don't have a lot of time.

2. Your statistics and accomplishments in your sport. You may also include your speed if it is very impressive, but you don't have to.

3. Academic and extracurricular accomplishments. For example, perhaps you volunteer regularly at a soup kitchen. Maybe you run the literary magazine. You may have won awards for your incredible artwork or your skills as a musician. All that information should go on this page. You should also have your GPA and SAT/ACT scores if they are available.

4. Think of your profile page like a very colorful resume. When I pitch the media, I give them something very similar. It is called a "one sheet."

Following, please find a sample profile page. You might want to spend about $100 to get a professional to design one for you. Have the designer use the colors in your travel team's uniform to really bring it together. Your travel team might even have someone whose job it is to create profile pages. If so, wonderful. If you are really good with layout and design, then you can make your own. Just keep in mind that a lot of information can look really crowded, and you don't want to go over one page. This is where a professional can really help you. Make lots of color copies.

You should carry around some copies of your player profile to all of your tournaments. A coach or a recruiter can hand them out to anyone who might be interested. One of my athletes had her older brother hand them out to coaches at a showcase. Although I am not quite sure about the NCAA ruling on this, it worked out very well for this particular athlete.

Sample Profile

Julianne Soviero #15

Pitcher/Right Field
Long Island Angels Travel Organization
2018 Graduation Year
juliannesoviero@gmail.com
www.flawlessfastpitch.com
Ward Melville High School
380 Old Town Road
Setauket NY 11733

GPA: 4.0
Intended Major: Psychology
SAT: 1700
ACT: 29
Height: 5'10''
Weight: 145
Throws: Righty
Bats: Righty
Pitch Speed: 63 mph
ERA: 1.06
Batting Average: .323
Home to first: 2.84
Home to home: 11.90

Athletic Achievements/Awards
2014/2015 All County Pitcher
2015 Pitcher of the year
2014-present Varsity Tennis
2015-present Softball Team Captain
2014-present Varsity basketball

Academic Achievements/Awards
2014-present High Honor Roll
2014 Joseph Broderick Medal
Ward Melville Young Artist Award
2014 Presidential Scholarship Award
Short Story Published in Scholastic

Extracurricular Activities
Editor of Ward Melville Literary
Magazine
High School Marching band
(Saxophone)

Community Service
Volunteer for Jacob's Ladder
Coordinator for Veteran's Appreciation
Day
Saint James Soup Kitchen Volunteer

Coach Contact Information
-Long Island Angels Manager: Joe Hennie
555-555-555
joe@longislandangelssoftball.com
-Pitching Instructor: Jane Doe
631-737-0196
juliannesoviero@gmail.com
-Varsity Coach: Jeanne Lalima
555-555-555
Wardmelvillesoftball@gmail.com
-Hitting Instructor: Rob Crews
555-555-5555
completegamesports@gmail.com

Some people also include National Tournament Participation in their profile page. I don't think this is necessary since the coaches will be getting a copy of your travel schedule, but you can include it if you'd like. Of course, I didn't have a picture of me in a travel ball uniform, since it's been a few years since I have played travel. Let me reiterate: YOUR picture MUST be in your travel ball uniform. You don't have to be smiling, but you can be. The accomplishments that I had written on the sample profile sheet are just examples. Don't feel discouraged if you don't have a million accomplishments yet. Include your own accomplishments and test scores and adjust the layout of the page accordingly. You can also include a team logo somewhere on the profile if you would like. I think that makes a lot of sense: it is easier for the coach to find the organization you belong to with some visual assistance. You will probably also notice that I included a website. I do think it is a good idea to create your own website if it is okay with your travel team and travel ball recruiter.

Connection Method III: The Phone Call

For most sports, a coach can't call you until sometime around your junior year. Even then, there are limits on when they can call you and how often. Here are some general guidelines:

Sophomore Year

College coaches cannot call prospects in any sport.

Junior Year

Men's Basketball: College coaches can call once per month beginning June 15th before your junior year through July 15th after your junior year.

Women's Basketball: College coaches can call you once per month in April, May and June 1-20th. They can also call once between June 21st and June 20th after your junior year. They can call again three times in July after your junior year (maximum of one call per week).

Football: College coaches can call once from April 15th to May 31st of your junior year

Men's Hockey: College coaches can call once per month beginning June 15th before your junior year through July 31st after your junior year.

Other Sports: Once per week starting July 1st after your junior year.

Senior Year

Men's Basketball: College coaches can call twice per week beginning August 1st.

Women's Basketball: College coaches can call once per week beginning August 1st.

Football: College coaches can call once per week beginning September 1st.

Men's Ice Hockey: College coaches can call once per week beginning August 1st.

Other Sports: College coaches can call once per week beginning July 1st.

<u>Division II</u>

All Sports: A college coach may call you once per week beginning June 15th between your junior and senior year.

<u>Division III</u>

All Sports: There is no limit on the number of calls or when they can be made by the college coach.

Here's the crazy thing: even though the coaches can't call you, you can definitely call them. You can borderline stalk them, although I wouldn't recommend it. The best advice I can give you is to call their direct line. If you are nervous to speak with the coach, write out a script of exactly what you would like to say beforehand. You can also write down any questions that you might have. If you don't get in touch with the coach on that first try, leave a message indicating the time that you will try back. It helps if you have some information about his schedule so that you don't call during practice or other team activities. This is the best way to get to speak with the coach. If you have called several times and left messages indicating the time you would call back and the coach is not around for ANY of those calls, he just might not be interested. Realize, however, that if you are not of age, he can't call you back. He is also very unlikely to be in the office over the summer, during college breaks, or while the team is traveling. Keep this in mind so you don't flood his inbox during a time when he won't get the messages anyway. This might also lead you to think that he is not interested in you when he really is.

So now you have a few different ways that you can contact coaches. DO NOT give up if you don't hear back the first time. Coaches are busy. They can't answer every email. They won't always be around to receive your phone call. Some coaches will even wait until they get several emails or calls from you before they respond. This is simply because they want to gauge your level of interest.

Connection Method IV: The Introduction

Let's go back to the dating analogy. You would probably be much more likely to go on a date with someone that your best friend set you up with as opposed to someone that your mom or your arch nemesis set you up with. This just makes sense: your best friend knows you, she knows what you are interested in, she knows someone who might be perfect for you . . .

You can probably see why introductions are by far the best way to connect with coaches.

I know that if Rob Crews makes a call on behalf of one of his A-Game Masters clients, that athelte will get taken very seriously by that coach. Certain travel organizations and/or private instructors are also able to make connections like these. They are trusted and respected, so college coaches rely on them for good information.

Conversely, bad travel organizations don't get any credibility, even when they are backing a legitimate all-star athlete. Maybe that girl that Aunt

Gertrude wanted to set you up with was a complete stud, but, you know, *it's Aunt Gertrude*. She always smells like 40 cats and is socially awkward, so what does she know about who might be good for you?

I think you get the picture.

You need to get some high-profile, trusted people backing you. If you can't find anyone willing to do this, take a good look in the mirror. Check your attitude or reasses your skill level. Why aren't high-profile people in your sport willing to make connections for you? Sometimes it is tough to ask yourself that question, but I have definitely had some pretty good athletes that I would NEVER introduce to college coaches either because they had horrible attitudes or their parents did.

Connection Method V: The Consultant

This is a huge loophole that many athletes are not aware of. Many Division I and Divison II Colleges have "consultants" working for them. These are people who are not technically assistant or head coaches, but are paid a consulting fee to work on a specific skill with some of the athletes in that program. As a result of the fact that these coaches are consultants, they are not asked to abide by the same rules as the people who are officially part of the coaching staff. This means that they often give private lessons. If there is a school you are very interested in, I would suggest seeking out their consultant and taking at least a few private lessons with him or her. If you are good enough, word will get back to the head coach. Sometimes, athletes who establish a verbal agreement are then asked to work exclusively with that school's consultant. They aren't always happy about it, but it is a good way to familiarize yourself with what will be expected of you and adapt to different teaching styles. Don't drop your current instructor if you are successful with him/her, but reaching out to a consultant can make a huge difference in your visibility to a college coach.

Chapter Review/ To-Do List

1. NEVER assume that a good coach will just find you. You must be proactive in your college search
2. Think of your contacts with coaches as "marketing yourself." Try to put together a complete picture of yourself and your achievements so that you prove you will be a tremendous asset to both the college and program. Your marketing campaign should be comprised of references, a skills video (sometimes), and a list of accomplishments (athletic and otherwise). Try to imagine that you are marketing the best product out there!
3. Make a profile page
4. One email and/or phone call is not enough!!!!! Coaches receive hundreds of emails each day. One call or email will not make you stand out. If you haven't heard from the coach after one contact, try again (and send snail mail as well). Also, remember that there are certain times when coaches cannot contact you or are traveling with the team. So don't give up unless the coach tells you that he or she would not like to receive any further correspondance from you.
5. Once a coach contacts you, follow up promptly!!!!!
6. Show that your atttitude is worth recruiting as well as your skill (See the chapter on managing your social media!!!!!).

Your homework before going on to the next chapter is to write emails or letters to AT LEAST five of the schools that you listed in Chapter Two. Look for clinics or camps for AT LEAST five of the schools you listed in Chapter Two. I would also like you to create a word document with all of the information in it that will eventually be on your profile page. Finally, start creating a list of resources who can help to introduce you to college coaches.

6 YOUR TRAVEL ORGANIZATION = YOUR AGENT

Somewhere along the line, someone probably told you that your travel team doesn't matter as long as you participate in good tournaments.

That person is either an idiot or someone who owns/runs a weaker travel team.

There are problems with playing on a travel team that is not well-established or well-connected. One issue that is constantly troublesome for weaker travel teams is that fact that, even if they go to good tournaments, they are on the fields or courts where no coaches will see them. It is really disheartening to pay so much money to travel and "get exposure," only to find yourself ignored on a field that is ten miles from the main complex. Are there ways around this? Yes. We will discuss those a little later in the chapter. In the meantime, let's discuss some things that you should be doing to help find the best travel team:

1. **Find out where former players have committed:** Check out any potential travel team's website and look at the "commitments" page. It might also be called a "student-athlete page" or "college corner" or something like that. This page will show you where the athletes who have played in that travel organization have committed collegiately. Remember the exercises I had you do earlier in the book to determine what kind of colleges you would like to attend? Compare that list with the different "commitment" pages. Are there a ton of Division I commitments when you are really looking Division II? Do you want to go Division I and aren't seeing any high level commitments listed? Then look someplace else. Most travel teams are very proud of where their players commit and they will display these commitments prominently. If you don't see anything you like on the "commitments" page, you can ask around, but chances are that the team just isn't that good.

2. **Find out which college coaches have been known to "run" practices:** Yes, this is a real thing. This often works out well for both the coaches and the players. Imagine that a coach from UPENN does a hitting clinic for your travel team. You will have an opportunity to attend this clinic. You will get to see her coaching style and she will get to see your abilities. You can even speak with her because, technically, she is running a clinic. Travel coaches who are good at networking often have coaches from different schools come to run some part of practice. On the other hand, many weaker travel coaches don't even realize this is a possiblity. I would recommend that you ask any travel organization that you are interested in about the how frequently college coaches run practice. It is also recommended that you find out specifically *which* schools have attended practice, since having a local technical college show up and tell you how to hit is probably not going to help you with your recruiting efforts.

3. **Ask about the team's "recruiter":** "What is a recruiter?" you might ask. This is someone whose sole job is to work as a liaison between college coaches and the players on the travel team. A recruiter is not a coach. Many travel coaches might claim that they can be both, but there is almost no way that this is possible. How is a travel coach going to mingle with coaches while you are competing? Your recruiter needs to develop a good rapport with the college coaches and promote you. There are times when this will have to happen while you are playing. That is why a travel coach is *usually* not an effective recruiter. I use the word "usually" because I have known one head coach over the years who works so hard contacting college coaches on behalf of his athletes that it wouldn't matter if he had a recruiter or not. He does all of this in his "free time," and has a great rapport with many different colleges. He goes above and beyond and is always focused on the progress and well-being of his players. He is the exception rather than the rule. In most cases, the coach should be focusing on coaching while the recruiter should be focusing on handing out

player profiles, getting coaches to come over and watch you play, and communicating with you to let you know who is interested and who isn't. A good recruiter can also save you time and money. If you are planning on going to a clinic and the recruiter finds out that the school hosting that clinic has no interest in you, you probably don't want to invest time and money there. If you still think that your travel ball coach can do all of this without a recruiter, keep in mind that many college coaches will not want to be conspicuous when they are out recruiting. They do this so that the athletes will not change their behavior when they know a college coach is around, but this can also make them hard to find. A good recruiter should be able to get the coaches to you when it matters. A coach can't do that while he is running the team.

4. **Avoid "daddy ball":** I'm not sure how common this expression is throughout the country, but in New York, it is very widely used. It basically means that the travel team is run by a player's father, which understandably creates a lot of problems. At a very young level, "daddy ball" is not such a big a deal, because scholarships are not on the line. At a higher level, "daddy ball" creates endless drama. No parent could possibly be objective about their child and the child's potential to play in college. There are going to be all kinds of biases and preferential treatment on a team like this. Run. Screaming. Now.

5. **Determine if you will get the playing time you need:** This is an important factor. If the team you are considering already has a stud in your position and you are just a backup, that might not be the best way to get seen, even if it is a really good team. Do your homework to make sure that you are not going to get either overused or underused. You won't play well if you are completely burned out, and you won't be seen if you don't play at all.

6. **Determine the quality of tournaments/showcases you will be playing in:** I am increasingly angered by the fact that everything is now called a showcase. There are absolutely no parameters on what constitutes a "showcase," and therefore, everyone calls their crappy tournaments "showcases." Good travel teams, unlike most parents, understand the difference between a good showcase and a bad one. You don't want to be wasting your money traveling to a

bunch of places where only one or two coaches are in attendance and none of them represent schools that interest you. Better teams also always end up on better fields. Look at the tournaments that your prospective travel teams have participated in, but also look at what fields that team has historically played on.

7. **Find out if the team is recruiting-oriented:** I think you know what I mean by this, but some travel teams are focused on getting all of their players recruited while some teams are focused on having fun and playing in tournaments. Both of these can be good things, but make sure you align your team with your values. Teams that focus on recruiting will usually help you to make a profile page and/or a video (if necessary).

When I do seminars on recruiting, this is inevitably the part where someone mentions how she is happy with her travel team, but realizes she has chosen a bad organization for purposes of being recruited.

What's an athlete to do?

You don't have to leave your current team if you are happy. You just need to keep this in mind: the less work that your travel team does, the more work you have to do.

For example, one of my most beloved clients of all time was clearly a Division I-quality athlete from the start. She played on a small 18U travel team from the time she was about 14 and was very comfortable and successful in that environment. She wasn't going to change teams. So instead, her mom became her full-time "recruiter." She would give me weekly updates about the contacts they made, the clinics they attended, and anything else pertaining to her pursuit of a collegiate career. During this athlete's junior and sophomore year, she probably went to a clinic or showcase every weekend. She and her family wrote tons of letters, made tons of phone calls, and had me to help. She ended up with a nearly full scholarship to a Division I school.

You can also research guest-playing on stronger teams or teams that are in closer proximity to the schools you are interested in. Guest-playing simply involves contacting a travel team and asking them if they would like you to step in occassionally when they need a player. This often works well for everyone, since many travel teams don't have their full roster every weekend. Graduation and prom both create a huge need for extra players. One of my athletes guest-played frequently when she was considering going to college in Texas. She lived in New York, but contacted Texas teams and let them know the weekends when she would be available. When she knew that she would be guest-playing, she would contact a bunch of Texas colleges and let them know that she would be in their area. This did get the attention of several Texas teams, even though she ultimately decided that she wanted to go to school in New York.

So basically, if your travel team isn't that strong, you need to guest-play for stronger teams AND you need at least one parent working almost full-time to do all of the research, scheduling, and contacting for you. If you think this seems totally overwhelming, it is. That is exactly why the A-Game Masters Program exists. In this program, an A-Game Consultant works with you and your family until you graduate. This Consultant will help you with the recruiting process from start to finish. He or she will also be a liaison between you and college coaches. So you can either:

1. Have a competitive travel team that performs all of the duties discussed in this chapter
   OR
2. Get your whole family involved. Start contacting schools, map out all of the clinics and camps you will attend, and start guest-playing on stronger teams. Keep in mind that to do this correctly will probably require at least 15 hours a week in research alone.
   OR
3. Do an A-game Masters program.

I think that all of those options work well, honestly. I have seen people get recruited by using one of those methods or all three. Also, keep in mind, it isn't "all or nothing." Playing for the world's best travel team doesn't guarantee you a scholarship. You still have to put in time and research. Similarly, an A-Game Consultant is not a magical wizard. You and your family will still have to be engaged in the process. I suggest that you sit down as a family tonight, and create a game plan based on this chapter. You just have to decide what works best for your family both financially and chronologically. If you are very young, you might decide to do the bulk of the work as a family unit. That will probably work out pretty well, although I would strongly recommend an A-Game Initial Consultation to get you on the right track. Joining an elite travel team or being accepted into the A-Game Masters Program will both look like very expensive options initally. When you look at all of the money you could potentially waste, however, these can sometimes actually be the more economical options over the long term. A bad travel team is still going to wrack up lots of fees, plus you will have to cover the cost of staying in lots of hotels (mainly at tournaments where there aren't any coaches). Additionally, the actual cost of college has become staggering. If an organization or an individual can help you to even get a small amount of athletic assistance, trust me, you will be much better off spending a few grand initally to avoid spending several times that amount down the road.

Chapter Review/To Do List:

1. When looking for a travel team, look for a strong "commitment" pages, a strong travel schedule, a good rapport with the coaches, and an appropriate amount of playing time.
2. If your travel team isn't very strong but you do not intend to switch teams, you can: guest-play, have a family member act as a full-time live-in recruiter (remember, that family member can't do everything that an actual recruiter can do, because they would be in violation of NCAA guidelines), and/or do an A-Game Masters Program.

Your homework before going on to the next chapter is to sit down with your family and discuss what options would be best for you. Also consider what will be most realistic for you. Weigh the pros and cons. If you are one of several siblings, your parents might not be able to invest several hours a week helping you with college research. That's okay, and that certainly doesn't make them bad parents. It just means that you need to modify things somewhat. Remember, you can do all of the things suggested in the chapter or only a few of them. Use the chart on the next page to help you get started:

	Cost	Weekly Time Commitment	Pros	Cons
Elite Travel Team				
Standard Travel Team				
A-Game Masters				
Family "recruiter"				
Guest-playing				

Julianne Soviero

7 MAKING YOUR VIDEO (OR NOT)

For some reason, everyone makes a big deal about the college video, except for college coaches. So let me preface this chapter by emphasizing the fact that it is *way* more important for you to be on a good travel team and attend a lot of good clinics then it is for you to have a $2000 video. If you belong to a strong travel team, the travel team might even do your video for you. That's a really nice bonus, but, truthfully, almost all of the athletes I have had sign to elite Division I schools never even made a video. They verbaled before it would even be reasonable to make a video. How did this happen? If you have been reading all of the previous chapters carefully, you probably know, but here is what saved them from having to make a video:

1. They started very early. In most cases, 8th or 9th grade
2. They played for elite travel teams and guest played for other great teams
3. They attended a ton of clinics at the schools they were most interested in
4. They had one parent taking on the recruiting process as if it were a full-time job
5. They often called coaches as opposed to just writing to them
6. Though technically coaches could not contact them at such a young age, they had someone act as a liaison for them (either a travel coach or an A-Game consultant).

So if you do all of that AND you are talented, you probably won't even need to make a video. If you are a little late to the parade, however, you will probably need a video, because these coaches haven't yet seen you in games, clinics, and practices.

Videos are typically very expensive, which is why it would be nice to not have to make one at all. Expect to pay around $500-$1000 or so for someone who is experienced and can do some good editing. Unfortunately, there are unscrupulous people out there who might tell you that they are familiar with your sport and can do your video, when, in fact, they are just lining their pockets. I have had athletes pay $500 or more for videos that were not fit to be sent out to any college coaches. You do not want to make this mistake.

I don't personally create college videos, but I charge a fee to critique and/or consult while a video is being made. I tell my clients what they need to include, cut, redo, reorder, and edit. I often advise my athletes to make their own videos initially. Believe it or not, some of the best videos I have seen have been homemade. After making a homemade video, you can determine if you really need a professional or not. This has several advantages:

1. It saves so much money (even after my consulting fee).
2. Even if you decide not to use it, you can get an idea of what angles make you look the best. You will also know what angles are not flattering to your form and/or your abilities.
3. These videos resonate with college coaches. Coaches don't want something is overtly edited or fancy. Oftentimes professional videos have too many "bells and whistles." You wouldn't want to give someone a fancy dinner when all he really wants is pizza.

Talk about how you would like to make your video with the people whom you trust. See what will be most realistic for you. If you don't have some decent recording equipment, for example, a homemade video is probably not a good idea. If you don't have a program on your computer that can do some editing, a homemade video is going to be a problem.

Regardless or whether you are making your video or hiring someone else to do it, here are some things to avoid:

1. DO NOT include a lot of edits in the interest of making yourself look perfect. That is a huge turn-off for coaches. As a friend of mine, who is a college coach, has stated, "even I could make 1 out of 100 screwballs look good!" What I stongly suggest is that you use the changing of camera angles to create a natural opporunity to edit. For example, coaches will want to see your drop ball from

both behind the pitcher and the catcher. Throw a bunch of drops with the camera behind the pitcher. Once you get 3-5 in a row that are pretty good, stop and then film from behind the catcher. You can edit out the bad pitches that came before and after the three gems in post-production. You can do the same thing with free-throws, shots on goal, or serves. It is simple and effective. Most editing programs will allow you to just cut that little bit and, before you know it, you will have a masterpiece that doesn't look like it was edited at all. Please don't make the mistake of showing only one repetition of each pitch or skill. A coach will not be able to get any sense of your ability this way. Show him that you can perform the skill consistently.

2. DO NOT make it so absolutely everything is obsessively perfect. Coaches will want to see your misses too. For my athletes, if they throw a pitch with great movement that is in no way a strike, I tell them to leave it. Let the coach see how much break you have. Let them also see how you respond to that missed pitch. I remember watching a video once and commenting, "this girl has an attitude every time she misses." I wouldn't want to recruit a girl like that, but some coaches might. Your video is a good time to show how polished and composed you can be, but coaches understand that no one is completely perfect.

3. DO NOT include music. I don't know who first thought of this, but it is distracting and coaches don't like it at all. For pitchers, my observation is that music also detracts from the sound of the ball popping the glove. Some coaches are auditory and will want to hear how your pitches come in.

4. DO NOT include game footage. If the coach is interested, he or she will come to see you in your game.

5. DO NOT try to be overly cute or creative. For pitchers, do a series of pitches (like drop) followed by another series of pitches (like curve). Don't go jumping around and making the coach decipher what pitch you are trying to throw when. It is an organizational nightmare and completely distracting. Label your pitches/skills or have someone audibly narrating the pitch you will throw or the skill you will perform.

6. DO NOT go to someone to do a video who does not have a proven track record. It is okay to ask someone how many athletes

he has had go Division I or II if he is charging $500 for your video. Some people are really just in it for the money and don't care about where you go to school. Unfortunately, I feel there are a lot of these types out there. If you are going to pay for it, it better be spectacular.

7. DO NOT turn coaches off with bad camera angles or bad quality footage. Good angles are essential! Make sure that your delivery and the result of your delivery are both visible. Make sure that there is good lighting and that you are not giving the coach a video that plays all fuzzy. If you are not sure what angles will work best to highlight your abilities, play around with different "practice" recordings to see where your form and power shine the most. If you are a pitcher, DO NOT cut off the plate. We need a good sense of your movement and speed relative to where the batter would be standing. I am also not a fan of saturating the colors in the video or doing a lot of slow motion shots. If this is what the coach asks for, you can do it. Otherwise, keep it simple.

Keep in mind that you will be making a video that is not only unique to your sport, but also to *your* position in *your* sport. Look specifically at what coaches in your sport want. I know exactly what softball coaches are looking to see from pitchers, but I couldn't tell you the first thing about what ice hockey coaches want. Your travel coach or specialty coach might be able to guide you here, but if he can't, you need to do your homework. There are a lot of examples of videos online, but that doesn't mean that the videos are good! Look at people who play YOUR POSITION in YOUR sport that have been recruited at a very high level. Even if you don't want to play at a high level, you should always be looking to film your best. Remember, coaches do have a network. So it is possible that a Division I coach sees your video, and you are not a good fit for that school, but they might refer you to someone else. That is why it is so important to make a good impression. Take your video seriously and create a quality product.

After you send out your video, some interested coaches will respond by asking you to come to a clinic, which you should then treat like a tryout. Other interested coaches might respond by going to see you play. Occasionally, a coach will respond by asking for a second video. Sometimes, they will want this video focused on a very specific skill. The head coach from a Division I program that I was very interested in asked me to do this. She requested a second video focusing exclusively on how I transitioned from fastball to change up. The video wasn't even two minutes long, but that was what she wanted. Don't be upset by a similar request. A request like this doesn't mean that your first video is bad. Oftentimes, it just means that the coach wants a little more information about you (which is never a bad thing).

There are other reasons why a coach might want a second video. If you intitially made your video at a young age, for example, she might want to determine if you have developed as a player. Coaches will also request more video footage to see if you have worked on specific skills that they have asked you to work on (like footwork, for example). If a second video is requested of you (or even a third), there is typically no need to hire a professional unless you are abysmal with technology. Instead of hiring a professional, ask the coach who requested the video specifically what she is looking for in terms of skills demonstrated, camera angle, and length. If you can cater to the coach's specific requests, she will know you are a good listener *and* a good athlete.

Now that you know what you SHOULD NOT do in your video what SHOULD your video include?

1. For any skills video, you should be wearing your travel ball uniform and look very well-kempt and composed. Begin with a brief introduction. Athletes used to look at the camera and do the introduction verbally, but it is becoming more and more commonplace to just put all of the necessary information on the screen for the coaches to view for a few seconds. This is a great option if you are shy. It is an also a great option to help you keep your video short. If you choose to speak your introduction, you should be articulate and poised. You will say your name, your year of graduation, your intended major, your high school, your travel team, and any major accomplishments. If you would prefer not to speak, then all of that information can just appear on the screen instead. Regardless of which method you choose, you should always include some written contact information, so that the coach knows how to get in touch with you. If you write your introduction, please check your spelling and grammar. Your introduction should be very short and sweet, but make your voice and/or writing is easy to read or understand! I have watched so

many videos where I have had to replay the beginning. Don't make life difficult for your prospective coach.

2. Your video should not be very long. Different coaches like different lengths, but they are all busy, so I would say you are pushing the envelope if you go too much longer than six minutes. Some coaches say that they prefer three minutes.

3. Showcase your best skills first when you put the video together. Most coaches won't watch your entire video, as short as it may be. This doesn't mean you have to necessarily film your best skill first, but it should go first when you do your editing. For example, I had one athlete whom I was working with many years ago whose best pitch was a curve ball. I went to the filming of her video to help her, and her curve ball was horrible that day. Of all days! We spent way too much time trying to fix it, which ended up tiring her out and leaving her feeling distracted about her other pitches. Instead, now I make sure that, if a pitch or a skill isn't up to par to start out, do it last. You will be changing angles in your video, so you will be able to edit the skill back in when you need to.

4. Always put your weakest skill last or leave it out entirely. The video is supposed to showcase your abilities, so I always recommend that you record everything, and then you can edit it out later if you'd like. For example, a few years ago one of my juniors had just learned a rise. She wasn't very confident in it, but I told her to go on and film it anyway. It ended up coming out so wonderfully that she put it first! Go figure! Stuff like that does happen, so don't be afraid to film everything and then just leave out the stuff that doesn't go well.

5. Make sure that you have exclusive access to the field or facility where you will be filming. You don't want to start filming your video only to find out that marching band is praticing with the archery club in that area that day. The coach viewing your video should not have to deal with a million distractions (or even one distraction, for that matter).

6. You will be surprised how long it takes you to make your video. This is not at all unusual. You might end up cutting down two hours of shooting to 5 minutes. Prepare yourself for this. If you

are not well-rested and you have not eaten, you are not going to perform your best. If you need a little help figuring out how to perform your best, please read, *Unleash Your True Athletic Potential.*

7. You can cut down the amount of time it will take you to film if you use two cameras simultaneously. This is very helpful, but you will still have to make sure that you have gorgeous angles. With two cameras, you will also probably need to spend more time editing after you are done filming.

8. If you have to do your video on two different days either because you are exhausted or because you were having a bad day, make sure that the conditions and time of day look the same so it doesn't look like it took you 30 days to do one five minute video.

9. Make sure that all of the other athletes in your video complement your skill set. I have been at more than one video where the catcher dropped several key pitches. OMG, you have got to be kidding me! Even if you have to hire a college athlete to come and complement your skills, it would be way better than having to shoot the same thing over and over because your catcher can't frame.

Things that pitchers need to include:

1. You should begin with your fastball and show it from several different angles. The front (from directly behind the catcher) and back angle (from directly behind the pitcher) are the most important, but I also like to include a few from the side (next to the pitcher). From the front and the back you need to make sure that you are hitting your spots and popping the glove. From the side, you are demonstrating your form. Not every coach will look at this angle, but I certainly would. I would be checking this angle for any potentially illegal pitches or any tendencies that might lead you towards injury later in your career.

2. You must hit 3-5 good pitches consecutively before changing angles. Coaches realize that there are editing tools out there, so you must make it seem as though you haven't edited anything. Consistency is the key, and getting several

consecutive working pitches for all of your pitches can take a really long time. Therefore, be prepared to spend a lot of time filming, and then be prepared to spend a ton of time editing. The editing will allow you to cut all that footage down to about five minutes. In order to facilitate better editing, once you hit 3-5 good pitches in a row, stop and change angles. Edit the bad pitches that came before and after the three gems. Then repeat that method on the next angle or next pitch. The change of angles and pitches will make the edits undetectable.

3. Do your "best pitch" after the fastball and film it from the different angles. Your best pitch may vary from day to day. If your curve is normally best, but it stinks the day of your video, move on and then come back to it. You don't want to tire yourself out.

4. I suggest warming up a pitch, then filming it, then warming up the next pitch, and then filming that. The reason I suggest this is because it might take you so long to get all of the correct angles on a change up that your other pitches might actually not be warm anymore. For this reason, it is best to do them one at a time.

5. Try to do the pitch that you are least comfortable with last (unless that pitch is the change-up, which every coach needs to see) or leave it out entirely. Remember that coaches might not watch the whole video and so you want to make sure that they see your best stuff first. Don't be offended, but when I had to watch videos for a school I was consulting for, I knew within the first minute and a half if the girl had what we needed. When coaches receive so many videos, they will be very selective with the videos they continue viewing. Put your best foot forward. You only have one chance to make a first impression.

6. Put batting and fielding AFTER pitching if pitching is your primary position. Please don't show a hundred repetitions of you hitting off of a tee. No one gets any benefit from that.

7. You can edit the video so that the coach has the option of selecting what pitch he or she wants to watch. For example, there would be a main menu in which the coach could select "change up" to watch first or "hitting" to watch first. This will provide a method for easy viewing. Remember, we want to make things as easy as possible for these very busy people!

8. Watch the video carefully before sending it out (or you can pay me to watch it). Make sure it includes everything that you need and want. So many athletes have a tough time getting recruited because their first videos are terrible. You are very unlikely to get a second chance here. Make this one count!

Finally, you should be able to send out a hard copy (on DVD) if asked. Some athletes only have a website or link and, though this may be easier for most coaches, some coaches might be more likely to view something sitting on their desks. It depends, so ask each individual coach what she would prefer. You want to make sure that you are able to be accommodating.

Remember, NO coach will ever offer you a scholarship exclusively based on your video, but it will be a way to pique their interests and show your skills. If you are doing everything else right, the video is nothing more than a coming attraction to get coaches to come and see the main event.

Chapter Review/ To-Do

1. Determine how you would be most comfortable doing your video and when. Will you get a professional to film it? If so, who? Make sure that anyone whom you could potentially hire is both experienced and trustworthy.
2. Do your video early enough so that the schools you are interested in are going to have a chance to see it before they are done recruiting for your year. If you want to play Division I, for example, that video has to be done way before your Junior year.
3. Showcase your skills in your video, but don't be afraid to include a mistake or two.
4. Look at examples of successful videos for your sport and your position. A successful video is something that led to a athletic scholarship.
5. Create a strong introduction where you are wearing your travel ball uniform.
6. Put your strongest skills/pitches in the video as early as possible.
7. Leave out your weaker skills/pitches or put them last.
8. Keep your video very short (around 5 minutes).
9. Consider using two cameras to cut down on the amount of time you spend filming.
10. Be prepared to send both digital files and a hard copy of your video. Ask the coach what he would prefer.

8 MAKING IT OFFICIAL

At this point, you have hopefully been in contact with several coaches. You should be thinking about scheduling visits to the schools you are interested in. There are two different types of visits: the Official Visit and the Unofficial visit. In either case, you typically get to spend some time with the coach and/or the team. There are some major differences that you need to be aware of, though.

- **The Unofficial Visit**: On ANY Unofficial Visit, you will be paying your own money to fly or drive to the campus, stay in a hotel, and get meals. Unofficial visits happen prior to your senior year, and it is your responsibility to cover any costs associated with them. You may have an unlimited number of these. Essentially, if you want to fly all over the country looking at different schools on your own dime, that is completely fine. In your contacts with different coaches, you would typically say something like, "I am interested in both the academic and athletic programs at your school. I would like to set up an Unofficial Visit during a time when you would be available to discuss your program with me." If the coach has no interest in meeting with you for an Unofficial Visit, she is probably not very interested in general, so this is a good way to gauge where you stand with any given school.
- **The Official Visit:** It used to be that this could ONLY happen during your senior year. Now, some of my athletes who are looking at Divison II and III schools are doing Official Visits in their Junior Year. Keep abreast of this, because rules do change constantly. On an Official Visit, the school pays for the entire trip. You are only allowed to do five Official Visits. That's it. This is very important information for you to know because you probably have a list of about 15 schools that you are interested in. You can look at all of those schools on Unoffical Visits but YOU CANNOT go for more than 5 Official Visits. Don't waste one of

your Official Visits on a school that you really aren't very interested in. I personally went on three, but had been on a ton of Unofficial Visits. I didn't need all of the Official Visits I was allowed because I knew exactly what I was looking for. Here are some things that typically happen on an Official Visit:

- o The coach will assign a player to you for the duration of your stay. This means that you will stay in that player's dorm room and participate in any classes and/or social activities that she participates in.
- o The player to whom you are assigned typically has a stipend to cover any activities you might do, but if you are staying there on a school night, you probably won't be doing anything too adventurous.

- Things you should do during your Official Visit to get the most out of it:
  - o **Try to make sure that you see a class in your major.** Go to the class. Try to learn and try to participate. Is this a learning environment you could see yourself being successful in? I know I would not have flourished in a place where the class sizes were enormous, so I ended up participating in a class of about 3 people on one of my Official Visits. I didn't end up going to that school, but it was in my top two.
  - o **Watch or participate in a practice.** Depending on the division, it might be possible for you to actually participate in a practice, but if you can't, watch the coaches interactions with the team and watch how the team interacts with one another. This is an important dynamic. The team will be your family for four years. Do you like the drills that the coach uses? Do you like/agree with his instructional style?
  - o **See what the team is doing for conditioning/weight training.** When I went to shadow Brandon Marcello at Stanford several years ago, I loved the weight training and conditioning programs that they did. The programs were specified to each individual player and they were so dynamic and unique. I also loved the coach there at the time. After watching several practices, I can tell you that I would have gone there in a heartbeat if I was still in high

school. I have seen other coaches and trainers that haven't been knowledgable at all and therefore were putting their players at a greater risk of injury. You will easily be able to determine if this is the case if you pay close attention during your Official Visit.

- o **Ask the other players what they think of the coach, program, and school.** I got very honest answers when I asked these questions. You would be surprised how much information the players are willing to share.
- o **Be smart about what is offered to you during your Official Visit.** During one of my Official Visits, the player whom I was staying with offered me drugs. That was when I decided that there was no way that I was going to that school. Until that point, it was in my top three. I didn't want to be in the kind of environment where my teammates would behave like that. In some cases, I have heard that coaches encourage their current players to offer potential recruits banned substances. After the Official Visit, the players report back to the coach about how the recruit reacted. It really becomes a test of your character. Don't take risks you don't have to take here. It makes no sense to drink, do drugs, or engage in promiscious sex on your official visit. There is too much at stake and no coach in his right mind would ever want to recruit someone who engages in that kind of behavior.
- o **Try to eat in the cafeteria at least once.** For me, this would be extremely important because I am vegan and not every school would be accommodating of this lifestyle. You might be paleo, or gluten-free. You might also have a severe food allergy. You need to make sure that the cafeteria isn't cross-contaminating food if that is the case.

Whether your visit is Official or Unoffical, you should have an opportunity to sit down and speak with the coach at some point. You will want to think of some questions for him so you can know as much about the school as possible and make an informed decision. You should make your own questions based on what is important to you, but here are some examples:

- ❑ What kind of support do you provide us with academically? How many nights a week are we required to attend study hall? Do athletes get to schedule classes first to accommodate travel? How much traveling will we do? Will I be forced to miss class frequently?
- ❑ What kind of weight training program are we prescribed? Are we expected to do weight training in the summer prior to freshman year? What are your expectations for the off-season? How many fall tournaments are typical (if it is DIII, there is only one)?
- ❑ On one of my Unofficial visits, I asked the coach where I fell in terms of her top recruits. She said that I was one of her top ten. I then made the HUGE mistake of asking about the walk-on process. Live and learn. She must have thought I was in love with the school then and there and really didn't go into scholarship negotiations. I later found out from somone who had transferred out of that program that they had a reputation for attracting a lot of good players, getting them to come to the school, and then cutting or benching them and only using the scholarship athletes. I was so happy to have avoided that fate!! Some schools do have a reputation for doing this, so look for the warning signs. You are probably not going to play at a Division I or II school if you have to walk on. Don't kid yourself.
- ❑ If this is one of your top choices, you can ask, "what kind of financial package would this university be able to put together for me?" Wording is important here. You can also use the offers from other schools as a point of VERY DELICATE negotiation, but don't be overly aggressive.

Chapter Review

1. You can have an unlimited number of Unoffical Visits, but you must pay for them yourself
2. You can ONLY have 5 Official Visits. Each will be paid for by the schools you choose to visit.
3. Use your visits to determine if the class sizes, program, and campus are really right for you. Pretend that you are a student at that school. Will you be happy? Be honest with yourself.

9 YOUR REPUTATION AND YOUR RESOURCES

Many of you have probably heard a story that you may or may not have believed, about an athlete who lost his scholarship because of something he posted on Facebook. If you are thinking that this sort of thing doesn't actually happen, you'd better find religion really fast. Oftentimes, a coach who is interested in recruiting you will assign someone to the task of looking at all of your online profiles, including Twitter, Facebook, Instagram, and Youtube. They want to make sure that they are recruiting the type of player that they think they are recruiting. So yes, scholarships have been lost because athletes were dumb enough to post pictures of them engaging in underage drinking and other unscrupulous behavior. Racist or sexist posts would be red flags for coaches too. Be very careful about what you post and the image that you are putting out to the world as a potential scholarship athlete. If you are not sure if you should avoid posting something, just DON'T POST. You are talking about the rest of your life here.

You also want to consider what kind of online social networks you belong to. I personally don't really belong to any because they just are a black hole for time, but if you want to do some online social networking, make sure it is for positive things. Maybe you are interested in helping the environment or volunteering at the special Olympics. These types of networks would be a much better use of your time than belonging to a Katy Perry fan group (although I don't think any coach would think less of you just for being a Katy Perry fan). Don't get into arguments or bullying on social networks. Everything is written there forever, so if it isn't positive or could get you into trouble in the long run, stay away!

The other thing that I strongly recommend my clients do is create a separate email account exclusively for contacting coaches. One of my clients did a very smart thing and made it her full name plus her graduation year. Brilliant! That makes it easy for the coach to see when you are graduating and it also keeps the email professional looking. I definitely wouldn't use an email address like sparkleprincess@imanidiot.com because you are really going to raise some eyebrows there.

By this point, you should really have a good idea of what to do and what not to do when it comes to college recruiting. You have also probably realized that you shouldn't go through this intimidating process on your own. You need a team of people who are going to help you. Here are the people whom I suggest for your "recruiting team" and what their roles should be:

Parents: Typically, I find it is best if one parent (the one who is able to interact best with others and has more time to commit to the project) really does all of the recruiting work. This might sound unfair, but you don't want there to be a lot of miscommunication going on. This could result in important information and/or deadlines getting missed because mom thought that dad was doing it and vice versa. For all of my athletes who have played at an extremely high level, they have always had one parent who has really committed themselves to the process as if it were a full-time job. Your parent(s) will:

- Help proofread the letters you write to colleges
- Help you decide what schools are most aligned with your interests
- Be your emotional support when this all gets tough (and it will get really hard at times)
- Drive you to different campuses and help set up time with academic advisors

Your parents WILL NOT

- Pick a school that supports their interests or their sense of "could have been"
- Do all of the correspondence and searching for you

Guidance department: The guidance department can sometimes be a huge asset and sometimes not. My guidance counselors were wonderful and sat down with me to help me figure out what schools would be suited to me. When I was down to my top two schools and really couldn't decide, my guidance counselor knew me well enough to say to me, "you know, I think you will be much happier near the city." Of course, she was right. I was very stressed at the time and she helped me to get some clarity. Even if your guidance counselor is totally clueless, though, he or she will still have to do some of the Clearinghouse stuff and send out your transcripts, so you need to develop a good relationship. Your guidance counselor will:

- Help you with your initial search
- Send your transcripts
- Help you with Clearinghouse
- Make sure that you have taken all of your Core Courses and
- Make sure your GPA is on track

A-Game consultant: A-Game is a network of coaches who have been around for a long time. Your A-Game consultant will not GET you a scholarship, because YOU will EARN a scholarship. He or she will help you to get your priorities straight and will use the huge A-Game network to find out what coaches are looking for your position in your sport. Your A-Game consultant can have many different roles. If you are only doing an IC (Initial Consultation) your A-Game consultant will tell you what level he thinks you will play at and what schools might suit you. He will also help you to understand exactly what you need to do to be ready for college academically. If you are an A-Game Masters Client, on the other hand:

- The network will act as a liaison between you and college coaches. They will provide introductions when appropriate, which is why the A-Game Masters Program requires an application.
- Your consultant will help you to find worthwhile clinics and showcases
- Your consultant will help you to guest play or advise you as to what travel team would serve your best interests
- The network will answer any questions you have about the recruiting process from the moment you sign up until the moment you are in college
- Your consultant will provide emotional support and encouragement when things get tough

Travel Coach/Recruiter: Your travel coach should typically be acting as a liaison between you and college coaches, but should also be getting you involved in the best showcases and tournaments. If your travel coach is well-connected, he can really do a lot for you. If he is not, or he does not get along with others, it can make the process very difficult for you. Your travel coach should also be pretty objective and able to tell you what level he thinks you belong at. He can sometimes make or break your college career, so choose wisely here!

Private Skills Coaches: This would be your pitching coach or someone who works with you on a specialty skill for your sport. If your coach is pretty good, she probably has coached many athletes who now play in college. She can refer you to them so that you can discuss their experiences and what they would/wouldn't advise. She can also give you a sense of what level she feels you belong at. She should be asking about your progress. From my standpoint, even if I have an athlete who is not an A-Game client, I still want to know how she is progressing in her recruiting endeavors. I'm just not going to do all of the work and research that I would for an A-Game client. Keep your skills coach abreast of everything that is happening with you. It is not unusual for a seasoned skills coach to ultimately make the connection that leads you to your scholarship. I have been happy to do this for many of my athletes over the years.

Chapter Review

1. Don't be an idiot about your online identity and what you post on social media. Don't post anything you wouldn't proudly show your grandma.
2. Make a professional email address that you will ONLY use for contacting coaches.
3. Develop your "recruiting team."

10 SIGNING ON THE DOTTED LINE

At this point, it is very possible that you have started some gentle negotiations with a school. If you are shy about asking for money, I completely understand. I am exactly like you. When one of my A-Game athletes finds her dream school and then wants to know how to broach the very delicate subject of athletic scholarships with the coach, I typically ask them to say something like this: "I really love your school, but my family and I are trying to figure out how we could make this work financially. Do you think you could give me some information in this area?" The other possibility is that you have already had offers from some schools, but perhaps not the school that you really want. In that case, you can say something along the lines of, "I am really interested in attending your university, but I just got an offer of $10,000 a year in athletic aid from Dowling. Dowling is another one of my top choices. Would your program be able to put together a similar package for me?" Obviously, you would tailor these statements so that you could feel comfortable saying them. I don't really recommend bringing up scholarships via text or email the first time you discuss the subject. I think it is important that you can hear the coach's voice. In some cases, hesitation might indicate to you that you are not their number one choice, but they would like to keep you interested.

There are two different ways to indicate that you have come to a financial agreement: a verbal agreement and the signing of your National Letter of Intent. Most athletes make a verbal agreement before they sign their National Letter of Intent. If you are looking at a Division III school or an Ivy school (where there are no athletic scholarships), your verbal agreement will allow the coach to "go to bat" for you in the admissions office. In other words, your grades alone might not get you into the school, but your grades coupled with your athletic prowess might. This is what academically competitive institutions offer in lieu of athletic scholarships.

VERBAL AGREEMENT
- Is NOT sanctioned or acknowledged by the NCAA.
- Is an agreement between the coach and the player. It oftentimes involves the player's family. Most athletic directors will also honor this commitment.

Here is an example of how a verbal agreement would work: let's say you love UNC State and they love you. You decide to make a verbal commitment for a percentage of your tuition. There is nothing binding about that, but it is frowned upon to still pursue other schools once you have made a verbal agreement. A coach with whom you have made a verbal agreement might find a reason to back out of it if you don't conduct yourself in a manner that is fitting for you as a scholarship athlete OR if you don't stay on track with your academics. Coaches don't regularly back out of verbal agreements on a whim, though. Most coaches are pretty ethical when it comes to that. If they aren't, they usually have a reputation. If you have made a verbal commitment and then decide that the school is not right for you, don't panic! Simply schedule some time to talk with the coach and let him know that the school isn't right for you. THEN you can go out and try to make a verbal agreement with another school.

Things to look out for:
- I am not really a fan of making verbal agreements where your scholarship would begin your sophomore year or your junior year in college. The coach might be telling the truth, but that means that you must sign your NLI without any financial assistance or guarantee. Once you are at the school, there is much less incentive for a coach to give you athletic aid. Basically, if your scholarship starts after your freshman year in college, nothing can be in writing for you, but you are committing to them. Are there cases where this works out anyway? Perhaps, but, to date, I have never seen one. Please just be careful.
- Stay away from programs where the coaches change from year to year. These are typically very unstable programs where you could have a coach that adores you one year and someone who wants you off the team the next year. Worse, you could make a verbal agreement with a coach you love, and when that coach leaves, the new coach could

decide not to honor it. Stability and consistency is important, especially when you will be spending so much time with your coaches and team. They are your family away from home.

- Stay away from coaches who seem to have inappropriate relationships with players. If the atmosphere is too casual and there isn't a solid distinction between the coaching staff and the players, trouble usually follows. This tends to happen particularly with very young head coaches. Good coaches care about their players, but keep it professional at all times.

- Stay away from coaches at very good Division I and II schools who want you to "walk on." A long time ago, there were schools that were getting a reputation for recruiting a lot of different athletes and then getting them to the school via a little bit of scholastic aid or similar. Then they would cut all of those great athletes but still have them at the school so that their competing schools couldn't get them. That is a terrible thing to do, but it happens. Make sure that a school is commiting to you if you are commiting to them.

NATIONAL LETTER OF INTENT

- This is a legally binding contract between the athlete, one parent/guardian, and the College or University's Department of Athletics.

- You can sign your National Letter of Intent in the 2nd and 3rd week of November for all sports except Football and Soccer (see the chart below to get an example of signing periods).

- The National Letter of Intent can ONLY be signed during your Senior Year of HS, there is no way possible for you to sign it sooner.

- The NLI is a written offer of Athletic Aid. It is only guaranteed for one year. Currently, rules are changing to protect student-athletes, but signing a document every year might be something that you have to be really careful about. A coach could possibly say to you that he will give you a 30% scholarship for four years. Here's the thing: you have to renew that scholarship every year. The next year, your Letter of Intent might indicate a 20%

scholarship. If you don't read your documents every time, things like this can happen and have happened. I have personally known coaches (whom I don't affiliate with anymore) who have done this on purpose to underperforming athletes. MAKE SURE THAT YOU READ EVERYTHING YOU SIGN!!!!

- Once signed, the National Letter of Intent is binding on the College or University, not a coach or team.
- Your college coach cannot be present at the signing.

Below are some recent signing periods for the National Letter of Intent. These dates were specific to 2013/2014, but the dates are always really similar. Notice that some sports have an early signing period and some sports only have a regular signing period. We encourage our A-Game athletes to be a part of the early signing period whenever possible.

NLI Signing Dates for Prospective Student-Athletes

Sport	Early Signing Period	Regular Signing Period
Basketball	November 13-November 20	Division I April 16-May 21 Division II April 16-August 1
Football (midyear JC transfer)		December 18-January 15
Football		February 5-April 1
Field Hockey, Soccer, Track and Field, Cross Country, Men's Water Polo		February 5-August 1
All Other Sports	November 13-November 20	April 16- August 1

If you are transferring:

First of all, I strongly recommend that you go step by step through this book so that you NEVER have to transfer. It is a mess both academically and athletically. If you do need to transfer and still want to play a sport, the first thing you need to do is get a "permission to speak" signed from your current coach. Don't be afraid to do this. Your current coach will probably be just as relieved as you are if things aren't working out. You MAY NOT engage in negotiations with any other coaches until this is done. Don't procrastinate!!!!!!!

Chapter Review

1. A Verbal agreement is a non-binding agreement between a player, that player's family, and the coach.

2. The National Letter of Intent is a binding agreement between the athlete, the parent or guardian, and the University's department of athletics.

3. Familiarize yourself with the signing dates for your sport

4. Your NLI is renewable every year

5. Read EVERYTHING you sign

Julianne Soviero

11 THE INSIDER'S VOICE: DIVISION I

Author's note: *I thought that it would be extremely important for you, as prospective student-athletes, to understand what it is truly like in Divisions I, II, and III. This is best explained through the words of the athletes who have been there very recently. Therefore, the next three chapters are dedicated exclusively to* their *voices. I have only edited for grammar. This chapter focuses on the Division I experience. Though the individual who experienced everything in this chapter prefers to remain anonymous, she is probably one of my most talented, hardest working athletes of all time. She really threw everything she could into playing Division I and I personally believe that she could have played anywhere she wanted to. She graduated college in 2014. This is her perspective:*

Playing Division I was a dream for me since I was 13. I knew I wanted to play at the highest level possible. When I was entering my sophomore year, my mom had a conversation with Julie regarding what level I would be best suited to. Julie felt very strongly that Divison I was the best fit for me, which was amazing because that meant that we were all on the same page. I began the recruiting process by looking up a bunch of camps and clinics at Division I schools. I knew I didn't want to leave the East Coast, so I did a lot of research and found all of the East Coast Division I schools that had my major and were hosting camps or clinics. My goal was to be verbaled by my junior year.

Sophomore year was when I really traveled . I went to camps and clinics at USF, North Carolina, South Carolina, Coastal Carolina, Chapel Hill, Villanova, Cornell, and many more. I did the camps because my travel team wasn't going to get me recruited. I loved my travel team, but they didn't showcase competitively or network with a lot of colleges. Basically, I couldn't rely on them to get me recruited. I had to take it upon myself to really get my name out there and make coaches come to see me. Looking back, I probably should have switched travel teams, but I worked hard enough to get recruited on my own.

Getting recruited was a full time job for us as a family: we sent materials out all day long and were responding to coaches' inquires all day long. My mom did so much work and would check in with Julie when she needed guidance or just wanted to update her on my progress. My dad would give us all input and help us plan where to go next. Mom and dad took me everywhere I could have dreamed of going to school. They took me to all of my tournaments in addition to all of that. I couldn't have done it without both of them.

When people ask me what it was that really got me recruited, I ultimately think it was my passion for the sport. I was so determined and passionate about playing Division I in College. It was practically all I could think about. That made my recruiting process a success. I wouldn't settle for anything less than Division I.

I realized that the hard work that my family and I were putting in was paying off at a tournament where there were about 15 coaches behind the backstop with radar guns. They were there to watch me and see how I performed live. I was a little nervous at first, but felt like it was such a wonderful thing and a step towards my dream. I had to try to ignore the pressure and give it my all. Hofstra, USF, Villanova, Elon, Hartford, and so many more schools were there: even other schools that I was never actually interested in! I was getting a ton of letters from D II schools and, though I was always polite with them, I didn't have any interest in playing there. I was really developing a good reputation among coaches at all different levels.

There was one Ivy League school in particular that was very interested in me. I sent the coach my video and he said that he was looking for a "number one" and that he wanted to come to see me pitch live. After he saw me pitch live, he let me know that I was his "number one." I was thrilled and really wanted to play there. Unfortunately, my SAT scores were under what I needed to go Ivy, but the coach and I had such a great relationship throughout the whole recruiting process that he referred me to several others schools when it became clear that there was no way I would be able to play at his school. That was what ultimately led to my scholarship.

I talked to a lot of different coaches, but the coach for the college that I ended up committing to just gave me a very good vibe. I felt comfortable with him and everything he was telling me about the program and the school. He had been there for many years and had run a pretty successful program. When I visited the school, I just had this weird feeling that I was supposed to be there. The pitching coach at the the time was someone I had grown up admiring. I thought about how amazing it would be to have her as my pitching coach in college. I had always wanted a male head coach. Oddly enough, on my unofficial visit, he had asked me what I preferred. I felt like it was meant to be. When I got home after my unofficial visit, I verbally committed.

I had a 90% scholarship to my dream school. Julie tells me that this is incredibly rare, as very few athletes get anything even close to a "full ride."

I signed my National Letter of Intent and my scholarship was set in stone. To my great surprise, only about two months after I signed, the coach whom I was so looking forward to working with said he was leaving. My heart just sank. Thankfully, the pitching coach whom I really admired was still going to stay. I was relieved since I felt like I would be spending about 90% of my time with her. Everything was going to be okay. Then a few weeks later she also said she was leaving. It felt like everything was falling apart. I had to wonder:
1) Am I going to be happy with this new coach coming in?
2) What if this new coach doesn't like me? I am not her recruit. She could basically ask me to leave.

I was anxious. I calmed myself down by thinking, "things happen for a reason." I knew I had no control over it. I loved the school and didn't want to go anywhere else. I felt that I would just handle it one step at a time.

Our new coach contacted everyone on my college team throughout the summer before I entered my freshman year. She seemed awesome. I thought, "maybe this will be even better." My freshman year was the best year ever. I loved it and was so happy and grateful to be playing DI. I even had a starting position my freshman year.

On a typical day, we were up at 5am to work out and then we would go to class. Sometimes we would workout, practice, and then go to class. On other days we would workout, go to class, and then go to practice. The whole day was booked and we were always up so early. It didn't phase me. I loved every second. It gave me this sense of fullfillment. While other students at the school were just waking up for class, I had already done so much. I would typically spend about 6 hours a day doing softball-related things. I would do this 6 days a week. Sometimes we had 3-4 hours of practice, an hour workout, and a half hour of conditioning. It would fluctuate a little. NCAA guidelines are there to make sure that Division I athletes only practice a certain number of hours a week, but there was a lot of "optional" stuff that wasn't really optional. Even on off days, we would usually still do some kind of workout, since we were all really committed to being the best we could be.

Balancing softball with academics wasn't easy, but I would give my professors our schedule at the beginning of the season and let them know what classes I had to miss. I had to communicate with my professors constantly to make sure that I was keeping up on my assignments. I had to keep them informed if there were rainouts or other things that would change the schedule I gave them initially. Some of them really didn't like the fact that I was missing class for sports, and that could be reflected in my grade. That is why it is really important to show your professors that you care just as much about your academics as you do about your sport.

Something that helped me to balance my academics and my athletics was the fact that my coach would tell us what time we would be practicing for an entire season. For example, we would practice in the morning in the fall. In the spring, we would have to take the classes in the morning, since practices and games were in the afternoon. This wasn't always a perfect system, though. Sometimes I had to take classes that I needed to graduate, which meant missing practice. Other times, there was no way around missing class. The NCAA has a rule that you need a certain GPA to be eligible. We had a team rule to maintain a certain GPA that was actually higher than that the NCAA's required GPA. If anyone on the team failed to achieve that GPA, she had to sit.

With all of the work I had put in, I was very proud to be a captain for both my junior and senior year.

As much as all of this seems like an absolute dream (and some of it was). It became like a nightmare for me.

Our coach became very angry and frustrated when we would lose, which was understandable. What was very difficult to comprehend was when she started attacking individual players for things that were not relevant to the sport. She started playing mental games. If I was doing poorly or just throwing the ball down the middle of the plate, I was already mad at myself, but I could understand where she might yell at me for something like that. That's just how some coaches try to push their players to get better. This was different. She would yell at me for reasons I couldn't even understand. For example, she came in when we were working out and made comments like, "I don't like your face right now." It was almost like she was testing us to see how we would react.

During my junior year, I had worked my hardest over winter break. I pitched several times a week and kept up conditioning and workouts. When I got back from winter break, she basically said that I sat on my ass and didn't do anything at all. She said that I really needed to prove myself. This was devastating. I would always come back from break and tell her how great I felt because I was working with Julie and was able to do so much with such confidence. Then my college coach would basically just break me down. I have never had any conflicts with any coaches or authority figures and I never ever had a mental issue with the game. I didn't really know how to react to this type of bullying. It took a toll on me both mentally and physically.

Physically, we were overthrowing. In all my years of pitching prior to college, I had only had one injury. At college, I was injured every single year, sometimes more than once. When I was injured, she would override what the school trainer and physical therapists would say, instead telling me that I needed to throw more. We threw 230-300 pitches a day. That had nothing to do with being in shape. Most good pitchers will throw under a hundred pitches in a game, but she had us doing two to three times that amount. If I struggled with that, she made me think that I couldn't hack it at a Division I level. For my whole career prior to college, I never thought about anything before going into a game. At that point in my career, I thought that I couldn't even throw anymore. That was the most disappointing thing for me. I had this idea of how I wanted to be in college, because I had always been so succesful, but it felt like I was so far from those goals.

An excellent example of a mental game she would play occurred when we were throwing live at practice for intersquad one day. I was doing very well. I was striking everyone out and hitting my spots and having fun with my team. To my surprise, I was called out into the outfield. She said, "what's wrong with you? There is a problem with you and you aren't telling me what there is." That made me doubt myself. Of course, then when I went back out, I had a horrible outing. I wasn't the only one that she did this to. Every day, one person on my team or more would cry. To be honest, I got the better deal because there are stories from my teammates that are way worse than what I went through. To this day, I can't figure out why she behaved this way. Everyone's performance only suffered with these tactics.

Once, when she felt that our locker room was messy, she called us all in, yelled at us, and then swung a bat as hard as she could into a locker, denting it. The whole team was in complete shock. Word got around and she was discplined for that, but the damage was already done. My team was so lost at that point. No one knew what to do or how to act. I held a meeting with my team as a captain. I encouraged them to really just focus on "us." We all wanted to go out and work and show everyone what we could do. Unfortunately, it was hard to do based on what was happening with our coach, and we had a horrible season.

Though my college career didn't end how I would have liked, I am so happy that I was able to play and compete at a Division I level. Here is my best advice to all of you:

1. You have to have a good feeling about the coaches immediately. If there is the slightest bit of doubt in your mind, it is time to reconsider. There are a lot of good coaches out there, but there are also a lot of coaches out there who can destroy you as a player and as a person. You might go to the college and find that the coach is not the person you thought that he or she was. Coaches can lie too, so make sure that you ask the players what the coach is really like behind closed doors before you commit.
2. Start really early. I wish I started earlier: even in 8th grade! The process can be very easy or very hard, based on how you prepare for it. If you are doing things at the last second, or you are unsure of the level you want to play at, it will be so much harder. If you are organized, prepared, and plan, it will go smoothly.

Good luck and I hope that you find the college of your dreams!!!

12 THE INSIDER'S VOICE: DIVISON II

Author's note: *The athlete who wrote this would prefer to remain anonymous and we will also keep the schools she attended anonymous. This athlete is extremely talented as both an athlete and a musician, which made her collegiate experience very challenging: she wanted to commit equal time to both. This athlete was recruited very early and at an extremely high level. She was one of my youngest athletes ever to verbally commit, which, as you will discover, is not always the best thing.*

Ever since I was eight years old, I had this idea drilled into my head: "if you work hard at softball, you can get a 'full ride' to college." With this phrase on a constant loop in my brain, I practiced about six nights a week and started private hitting lessons and private pitching lessons. I learned to eat during car rides, and to do homework through car sickness. This was a necessity since I lived on Long Island and I used to go to New Jersey and back for practice during the week. At the age of fourteen, I would sometimes go to California on the weekends and then take a red eye home so I could go straight to school.

Sleep was a small portion of my life, and my social life was a ball and a bat. There was no "after prom" because I had a game the next morning. I had no time for casual gatherings because I constantly had work I had to catch up on. With my time so strained, I had no time for error. I learned determination, drive, responsibility, the worth of money and time, and how to grow up rather quickly. Although at the time I wanted nothing more than to be a "normal" teenager, today I see the value in a lot of what I did. Part of me still wonders, though: were all those childhood sacrifices worth it?

My parents went into debt to pay for all the travel expenses and lessons, and now they watch me play at a level less than their ultimate goal. Of course my happiness is what makes them happy, but I have to watch them struggle. It breaks my heart knowing that I am not where they imagined me to be. I am not where I imagined myself to be. If only I knew beforehand the sacrifice, the reality, and the true meaning of college sports, I would have done things very differently. I also would have changed my parents' perception, and probably saved a lot of money, time, and stress. If I knew then what I know now, I could have had an amazing four years of college. Here is my story:

I was determined to make everyone happy, save money on college, and reach my maximum potential. I started training hard and playing for travel leagues at the age of eight. I often played up with the 16U teams at the age of twelve, knowing that experience would provide me with college exposure early on. Everyone convinced my family and I that this was the best thing for me. Now I understand how naïve we were. We went to Colorado, California, Jersey, Maryland, Pennsylvania, Virginia, the Carolinas, Georgia and many other states just to play in recruiting tournaments and combines. At the age of 14, I was putting a number on my jersey and pitching with a radar gun in front of me on a regular basis. My heart would be pounding out of my chest. I was usually overwhelmed at the end of a combine by the combination of my father, my coach, and a stack of papers. The papers contained information from all different colleges. I remember thinking: this is like a different language to me.

There was so much pressure on me at such a young age and I could barely understand what was happening. As a result of the fact that I did not know anything about colleges or what I wanted to pursue in life, my mother took it upon herself to manage my recruiting experience. The insanity and pressure on her was also ridiculous. She took responsibility for my adult future when I was only 14, knowing she could only guess at what I would want 4 years down the road. At fourteen, I did not know what I wanted, so how could she? How has it become commonplace for collegiate sports to recruit their prospects at such a young age? When you are that young, you are not ready to make a decision that will affect your career and the rest of your life.

I remember not even knowing which colleges I was heading to for my first unofficial visits. I walked into many fancy offices with impressive Division I coaches. With my hands shaking, I would listen to them ask me, "why are you considering this program?" My first instinct was to look at my mom sitting next to me. I had no idea! How did these coaches not see that they were asking a child questions that they should have been asking an adult? All I knew was that people told me I needed to play in a big stadium with hundreds of people watching me and ESPN filming me on television. Ultimately, those ideas consumed my naïve mind. During the recruiting process, I was completely forgetting the fact that college is an educational experience: I was only focused on softball. As I result, the school that I verbaled to seemed perfect at the time: it had huge stadiums, an outrageous campus in the middle of the country (which I thought I loved), Division I status, and great location. My mother also realized that I would graduate with an engineering degree from one of the top engineering schools. She convinced me I would make a lot of money and everything would be ok, and so we both thought I was making the right decision. We were in over our heads. The program, the campus, the coaches, and the elaborate Nike contract sold us.

When I was fifteen years old, I had to start the very difficult process of telling all of the other collegiate coaches who had shown interest in me that I would not be attending their schools. I remember feeling heartbreak that I had to turn down their offers and interests. Despite my excitement at attending my supposed "dream school," every day I questioned those other offers. I had an uneasy feeling in my chest: the heartbreak never seemed to ease. To this day, I can remember the exact place where I was standing while telling those coaches that I would not attend their schools. I remember the feeling that overwhelmed me. Was I really making the right decision at fifteen? How was I supposed to know? Today, of course I know my decision was wrong. It was all too much, too fast. It has lead me to the most stressful collegiate career I could have imagined. It has lead me to three different schools.

I will not lie: the school I verbaled to initially was actually the best school I attended. A typical student who knows what she wants to do and can enjoy the college experience will never regret going there. I definitely miss things about that school every single day: my friends, the atmosphere, the education, the different people from all over the world, and the experiences I had. Unfortunately, I gave those things up because I thought I was made to throw a ball. I felt that I was not getting a fair opportunity to do so there, so I had to move on. As a result, for an entire year my confidence level was at its lowest. At close to two hundred pounds, and with no background in weight training, I was not in the same kind of shape that my teammates were in. I was definitely not where the coaches wanted me to be. I developed symptoms of anxiety before conditioning practice: sometimes I would go into the bathroom and cry because I was so afraid. I would get on the line with the rest of the girls only to finish last. I was so disappointed in myself as I had to listen to each teammate come up and tell me that I needed to push myself. My coach would scream that the whole team had punishment runs for my inability to finish the run in the allotted time. I felt alone, disappointed, out of shape, and scared. I thought the whole team hated me because I was not as physically fit as they were, and they were punished for my ineptitude. I never wanted to punish anyone, I simply was not prepared for the intensity of Division I athletics. I was the youngest on the team with a late birthday, and I was looking around for some guidance but got none. My pitching began to suffer, my attitude began to diminish, the stress levels of being on the field were sky high, and the fun of the game was gone. I went out on the mound shaking like a leaf. I thought that if I even walked a single batter, my opportunity was over. There was no time to make mistakes and there simply was no direction. These coaches expected me to come in and produce immediately. All I did was fear the game, fear the ball, and fear all eight hours of practice a day.

Dreading softball was one piece of a very unhappy equation, but it was exacerbated by the fact that I have always been a little different from a stereotypical athlete. I am shy, quiet, and I mostly keep to myself. As a freshman in college, I had never consumed alcohol or been to a party. As a result, the other girls on the team perceived me as weird, stuck up, or not a "team player." Little did they know, I was more driven than any of them, but I expressed myself differently. I did not like to go out to the weekend parties and celebrate my victories. I would rather sit at a local theater and watch a show. This only alienated me further from my teammates. Every month I was called into the coaches office. I heard things like, "Your body language is terrible," "you show no emotion," "you do not smile," "you do not talk," and "you need to change." I did not want to change and felt like the coaches didn't understand me either. I started to miss the friends and family who understood my personality: I missed the people I could sit in a theater with on a Friday night. I wanted my team to be like my family away from home, but I was sadly realizing that there was no way that would happen. I made friends outside of the team but that was of little comfort because I traveled with the team all of the time.

My education also became an issue since I started my undergraduate education as an engineering major but realized that I missed music in my life. I decided to change my major to Music Education, which made everyone's heads spin. The coaches said it was impossible and the music department thought I was lacking focus because I spent more time on the ball field than in a practice room. Soon, I started to hate both of the things I once loved. I thought about quitting softball because I loved the school and had music, but it was more complicated than that. Playing collegiate softball was my dream, my parents' dream and ultimately the only way I could afford a degree. If I quit I would be letting down everyone who had worked so hard to get me there. So I made the decision to leave the campus I loved and try to find a Division I school near where I grew up: a place where I could be with my family and friends and escape the feelings of loneliness. To this day I regret leaving. Saying goodbye to that school meant leaving a lot behind. I wish I was aware that committing to high level collegiate softball meant being pigeonholed into a pool of majors and being sentenced to anxiety and stress.

I decided to transfer to a top Division I school near my hometown. It had a world-renowned music department and the campus was only twenty minutes away from where I grew up. When I was originally being recruited, I promised myself that I would never play for a local college team, but the crunch for time in the transfer process made this school seem like the only viable option. I had known the coaches since I was eight years old: I got training from them very early in my career, so I felt safe with them.

I never thought I could make the same mistakes again but unfortunately that wasn't the case. Since I had left a full ride behind in order to transfer, I decided to help save my parents' money by convincing the coaches to let me commute to school. This became the first problem the coaches had with me. My family and I never saved for college because we were all so sure that I would play my way through school. Transferring from a school that had given me a full ride left my parents trying to do all they could to spend as little money as possible. Since I only lived twenty minutes away from the campus, commuting seemed like a good way to help them out. Unfortunately, the fact that I didn't live on campus became a constant source of trouble.

Being a music major was once again an issue, since it is such a huge time commitment. Though the coaches initially said it wouldn't be a problem, the time that softball required made it nearly impossible to be successful in my studies. Once again, I wanted the team to be my family, but because I was different, I still felt ostracized. Just like the girls on the previous team, they called me weird, laughed at me, and told me that I was not a team player. I felt like much of this isolation was a result of the fact that I wouldn't go to the bars with them on the weekends. My collection of Division I college softball experiences made me think that Division I Softball was a cult, and you either join it or you get pushed out.

I got along well with the coaches on the field. I liked their intensity and how they pushed me, but there was no balance. We never talked about anything but softball and there were hours upon hours of practice, extra practice and 5:30 am conditioning. I went from having eight hours of practice a day to about twelve hours of practice a day, leaving me struggling to stay awake in class. I had no time to work on my performances, and so my grades were dropping and my professors were understandably upset. I was fearful of broaching the subject with my coaches, but I decided to talk to them about adjusting my schedule so that I could be successful in the classroom while playing. Let me remind you, the softball practice hours were going way over NCAA guidelines and making my studies nearly impossible.

After talking to my coach, I was disappointed at his response, which essentially encouraged me to stay up all night if I really wanted to excel in music. I was already getting home at midnight. After getting home, I had to do my written assignments and then wake up in three hours to go to conditioning. I wanted to physically be able to perform at the level that my coaches wanted, but I was finding that impossible. I was a transfer student taking 36 credits of music classes: over twice the amount of credits that a normal student takes. I had performance hours and shows, often running late into the night, and eight hours of rehearsal a day on top of twelve hours of practice. He was really telling me that I needed to choose between softball and music. I wanted to become the first student-athlete and musician at that university, but I was very disappointed that, for the second time, I was let down. My coaches just kept telling me that I couldn't do it. I started to feel that Division I was overrated and unrealistic. It was softball with no school. I decided that I could no longer do softball.

Though I found comfort in my music, this decision left my parents in a complete financial struggle. There was no scholarship anymore, so all of the money they had spent on travel ball and lessons was basically thrown away. To make matters worse, the softball world is a very small world and the things that people were saying about me got back to me very quickly. I was hearing things like, "we knew she wouldn't make it," and "she was not that good anyway." Nobody had any idea about what I had been going through.

My experiences at the Division I level had been mentally debilitating. I needed a new start. I decided to take a step back and stop getting in over my head with these childhood dreams of Division I softball. I knew I could compete on that level, but I needed to think about life beyond the softball field.

I decided to look at some local Division II schools. The Division II school I chose was "open-arms" as far as music goes. After my horrible experiences in Division I, I didn't know if I wanted to play softball again. Playing was too stressful: it wasn't worth it. Softball was supposed to bring me stress relief from school, but instead it made me more stressed than school itself.

The Division II school I chose had one of the best softball programs in the Northeast. It was close to home, but I still had the opportunity to stay on campus. The head coach was also very different than any coach that I had ever had. He sat down with me and made sure that I got all of the classes and credits I needed. He answered all of my questions without complaint. The first time I transferred, I was considered needy when I had questions. I would ask the Division I coaches about the next steps I needed to take in the transfer process and they acted like I was a burden. The Division II coach did everything he could to help me.

As a note to the readers, transferring is very difficult process because you have to make sure that your credits will be the same. English 101 in one school might not be the same as English 101 in another school. Transferring twice left me a year behind academically. It is also very difficult because you have to get "permission to speak" from your current coach. This can make a strained relationship even worse. In terms of playing at your new school or getting a scholarship at your new school, you are basically hoping that someone de-verbaled or is not performing well so that you can have a spot on the roster. Additionally, there are lots of rules about playing and transferring, and since I went from two Division I schools to a Division II school, I had to sit out an entire year.

In Division II, there is more of a balance between education and softball. I WANTED my time spilt equally from the beginning, and now I have that. At my Division II school, I get to miss games if I have to because I am first chair saxophone. That would never happen at either of the Division I schools. At my Division II school, if I have a game and I need to be a half hour late to class, my professors understand.

My Division II experience now is what I expected my Division I experience to be like. Now we train for a maximum of 5 hours a day and my coaches will work around my class schedule. I liked the intensity of Division I, because they leave it all on the field, but there is just much better balance in Division II.

During a typical day at my current school, I do early morning workouts by myself at 6 am. I sign in, run, and then lift. After that, I usually have 3 classes that are each an hour and fifteen minutes. Then I go straight to practice. Bull pens are usually during practice. Practice can be as long as 3 hours. After softball practice, I go straight to rehearsals. Rehearsals are 3-5 hours. They are 0 credit classes, but I need them to graduate. I typically get out of rehearsal at 8:30 and then get dinner, do homework, and pass out. As you can see, Division II is still not an easy schedule, but it is manageable and I have a lot more support. There was no one telling me "you can't do this."

Though all of the other schools promised me that my team would be like my family, the school where I am now is the first place where that is true. Lots of the other girls on the team don't like to drink or party. They accept me for who I am and make me feel like I belong.

I hope that my story helps at least one athlete out there to make a better decision about his or her collegiate sports career. I wish I would have chosen the Division II school from the beginning. It would have saved me a lot of self-esteem issues and maybe even prevented the crushing anxiety that I am still dealing with to this day. Don't let the beauty of Division I sports fool you. Think about your own sanity and happiness. Don't think about that "full ride." I actually had that at the first school I attended, but it wasn't worth it. Look for fulfillment and comfort. Allow yourself to have fun: that's probably why you started playing sports in the first place.

Julianne Soviero

13: THE INSIDER'S VOICE: DIVISION III

Author's Note: Julie McDonald wrote this chapter. She is a brilliant and talented young woman who could have played Division I or II if she wanted, but she chose Division III. You will notice that she started the process much later than the Division I and Division II recruits because there are no athletic scholarships at the Division III level. There are only verbal commitments. She graduated high school in 2014.

I began my recruiting process during the fall of my junior year of high school. My grades were always my top priority, so I had my sights set on academically selective Division III institutions. As I observed rather quickly, the major difference between DIII recruiting and DII and DI recruiting is the actual signing day. DIII only allows for verbal commitments, so there are no official letters of intent. However, almost every other aspect of the process is analogous to the DII and DI processes.

The first step that I took in my recruiting process was searching through the lists of college coaches that were at the showcases I planned on attending. Then I would email the coach of every school that I had even the slightest interest in, in hopes that I would receive as much attention as possible. After several showcases throughout my junior summer, my choices were narrowed down. During the fall of my senior year, I went on overnight visits to the few schools that had piqued my interest. I found that overnight visits were what really solidified my opinion of a school. That's when you see if you fit in with the team, if the classes are suited to your learning ability, and, most generally, if the school is a good fit for you.

After exploring all of my top options, I found myself unable to make a verbal commitment. The coaches I spoke to explained that, without a verbal commitment, they wouldn't be able to back me in the admissions office. This meant that I would need to get into the school based on my academic record alone. This was intimidating, but I was confident enough in my grades to get me in. I ended up getting denied to some schools that I would've gotten accepted to if I had made a verbal commitment, but my hesitance to commit showed me that those institutions weren't the places for me. Finally, in April of my senior year, I made a commitment to play at Wesleyan University, one of my top choices.

There's nothing I would've done differently during my recruiting process. I believe that I started early enough, maintained contact with all of my coaches, and showcased my skills. I was nervous about not being committed when most of my teammates were, but finding the perfect school is about more than just softball. After going on my overnight visits in the fall, I didn't feel that I had found the right place for me. I went on an overnight visit to Wesleyan in the winter of my senior year, and that's when I realized that Wesleyan was where I belonged. Two years later, I still feel the same way. I believe that the "gut feeling" that everyone talks about when you've found the right school is very real.

Now that I've experienced the life of a typical DIII student-athlete, I still wouldn't change a thing. My time at Wesleyan can be summed up by one word: busy. Student-athletes at Wesleyan are held to the same academic standards as every other student, while also having to make time for practice, lifting, and other team events. A typical weekday for me consists of lots of class, lots of studying, and lots of time at the athletic center. The routine is usually: wake up, go to class, get lunch, go to class, go to practice, get dinner, shower, and hit the library. This fluctuates with the amount of work I have to do in a week, but generally sums up my schedule. I also have a work-study job, so I fit that in when I have extra hours in a day. On the weekends, we usually have team events. We work at the football games and have other fundraisers. When I'm not doing something with the team, I'll usually sleep late, wake up and study until dinnertime. After dinner, it's finally time to forget the books for a while and have some fun with the team and my friends. It sounds like all we do is study, and while we do study a lot, it definitely does not consume our lives. I get eight hours of sleep a night, and I have plenty of time to go to the gym every day, keep my job, do my lab research, and go out. It's a lifestyle that's dependent on your own discipline to do your work, athletic and academic, when you need to.

By NCAA rules, DIII teams have significantly less team practice hours than DII and DI schools. Most DIII schools have only one game day in the fall. Going into my freshman year, I thought that this restriction would mean less time on the field and in the cage. I was wrong. I was at captain's practices (where the coach isn't present) at least four times a week, and our conditioning packet had us in the gym six times a week. What I've realized is that these NCAA restrictions don't mean less work, they mean that you, as a college student-athlete, are expected to have the discipline to work hard on your own. My team and my coach trust me to work hard every single day. I understand that for some, this atmosphere is not conducive to maintaining an effective practice routine. For me, it's perfect. It gives me the flexibility to work out when I want to so I can balance my other activities with softball. I've learned how to manage my time and self-motivate. And that's just in the off-season.

In season, we're just as active as any other school in the country. We practice every day, we have a spring training trip to Florida, and after that we have about 6 games a week. This is where the skills we practice in the off-season are crucial. For an academically rigorous school like Wesleyan, proper time management for an in-season athlete is vital. After practices or games, our team usually ends up together in a study room in the library. Also, we rarely need to miss class for games. When we do, our professors are generally understanding and allow us to make up the work. I've never had a problem with a professor because of an in-season conflict. Essentially, the most challenging part of being a student-athlete at a school like Wesleyan is learning how to balance classwork, practice, and extracurricular activities.

Throughout my recruiting process, I realized that Division III athletics are stigmatized as inferior to Division II and Division I. Admittedly, the caliber of play of DIII isn't equivalent to DII and DI. However, DIII athletics give you the opportunity to continue to play the sport you love while exploring career options, extracurricular activities, and opportunities to study abroad. I'm in love with the sport of softball, but I realize that if it consumes my entire life, I won't have the same chances to advance in my chosen field as I do at Wesleyan. Personally, I think for any academically driven student-athlete, DIII is the way to go.

Julianne Soviero

14 THE INSIDER'S VOICE: HIGH SCHOOL JUNIOR

Author's note: Though the author of this chapter, Sarah Mc Keveny, has only been taking instruction from me for a few months, it is clear that she is exceptional both academically and athletically. She is a very rare athlete: what I refer to as "unlimited." This means that she will not easily "max out." She will always be able to push more and break boundaries. For this reason alone, I think she would be invaluable to any collegiate sports program, but her academics take her to yet another level. It is extremely important for readers to understand that this young woman really is high-level Division I material, yet the recruiting process was still extremely challenging for her. Notice how often she has had to change her #1 choice. This is common in the recruiting process, but can be heartbreaking. Fortunately, Sarah's story has a very happy ending: a few weeks after writing this chapter, she verbaled with a very academically competitive Division I school.

I thought it would be easy. That was my first misconception. Throughout my athletic career, I have been told that I am "Division One material," over and over again. I thought the first coach that looked at me would see my potential and recruit me right away. Little did I know, the college recruiting process comes with a lot more rejection, stress, and self-doubt than I could ever have anticipated.

I started the recruiting process earlier than most. I went on my first college road trip the summer before eighth grade and sent my first email after my eighth grade Varsity season. At that stage of the process, I sort of just expected to receive an offer from a coach early in my high school career. I was hoping that I would never have to worry about the long and involved recruiting process.

The recruiting process is nothing short of an emotional roller coaster. I have never experienced so many mixed messages and so much rejection. I would even go so far as to say I have had my heart broken: twice. By tenth grade, I had my heart set on a Division One school which I was convinced was the perfect school for me. It fit all my criteria: geographically, academically, and athletically. It was a small, quaint school not too far from home. I wanted something that was away from home, but not too far, and this school was the perfect balance. The coach expressed a great deal of interest in me for over a year. He came to see me play and talked to my travel and private coaches. He had finally invited me to a camp on campus the summer after tenth grade: he wanted to see me play up close and personal. I played my heart out, and I was convinced he liked what he saw. He told me at the end of the first day that he was a big fan of my softball skills, my grades, and my attitude. His assistant coach even told me that they wanted to talk with me more and discuss opportunities for me to attend the school. I went back to the hotel that night smiling in excitement, confident that the coach of my #1 college wanted me!

The next day, I felt an uncomfortable vibe and my hope began fading. It seemed that the coaches weren't talking to me with the same level of enthusiasm. I was baffled as to what could have happened to dissuade their interest. When we talked after the camp, they informed me that they had already recruited too many pitchers, and they needed to focus on other positions in the next two years of recruitment. I was completely and utterly devastated. I wanted to throw up. This was the first heartbreak of my recruiting career. I thought that school was just the right place for me and I had channeled all my efforts in their direction. When I realized it wasn't an option anymore, I was stopped dead in my tracks. The importance of keeping all of my options open finally really hit me, because nothing is ever guaranteed.

After spending a few days upset about this heartbreaking experience, I decided to get back on the horse and started bombarding other schools I was interested in with emails. My #2 school quickly became my #1 school, as I sadly crossed my #1 school off of the list. I had previously attended a camp at my #2 school and was very pleased afterwards. The coach gave me most of the attention during the two-hour pitching evaluation. She never drifted more than 10 feet away from me, constantly watching and commenting on my performance. She offered me small fixes on my technique and complimented my speed and response to her corrections. She had told my coach how interested she was, and agreed to come watch me play at one of our tournaments. In the fall of 11th grade, she set up right behind the plate to see me play. I was pitching quite well against a very good team: I gave up very few hits, held them to two runs and recorded the win. After that game, she talked to my coach for what felt like hours. She had told my coach that she had narrowed down her 2017 pitching recruits to three people and was considering taking two. In addition to me, there was a player from California and one from Florida. Hearing this gave me mixed emotions. First, I was thrilled to have a 2/3 chance of being recruited. But I was also concerned because the other two candidates were from states that play softball year round, giving them a clear advantage over me. All I could do at that point was wait for her to get back to me regarding whom she had chosen. In the meantime, I continuously sent her updates on my school performance including my induction into a second honor society and a competitive athletic service organization. Each time I wrote her she responded. All of her feedback was positive, everything seemed good.

It was a long two months as I waited for her to make a decision. She had given a decision date, and I excitedly called my coach that evening. My coach tried his hardest to let me down easily as he told me that the coach had picked the other two girls to recruit. My stomach knotted as I heard the news. My second heartbreak hurt more than my first.

At this point, as a junior in high school, I began to worry that time was running out. I began doubting myself and thinking maybe I wouldn't play college ball. With my grades, I could probably go anywhere I wanted, if I didn't have to worry about going to a school where I could play softball. These thoughts swarmed around my head for a couple of weeks, until I realized there is no sense filling my mind with bad thoughts when I could be making myself better. I decided to continue to improve my skills and continue reaching out to D1 coaches. I was happy to learn that some D1 schools hadn't even begun recruiting my year yet. Giving up was not an option. I put myself out there again and accepted two other invitations to attend prospect camps for schools originally in my top 10. At one of these camps, I did not seem to pique the coaches' interest; but at the other, I did well and the coach expressed interest in me. Decisions remain to be made, though.

To be fair, in the midst of all of the heartbreak, there has also been positive attention. I did receive a D1 offer which I declined, because I had no interest in the school. A few D2 schools are seriously interested, two of them have made offers and I am currently considering both of them. After almost every showcase, even back to 9th grade, I receive interest from multiple D3 schools. Who knows: maybe one of them is the right fit for me?

As I reflect back on the last three years, I know now that academics is the most important thing to me, next to softball and geography. It is important to love the school that you choose, rather than just choosing to attend because of softball. Imagine if something terrible happens and you are unable to play softball anymore…it is important to love your school for this reason. Another thing I keep hearing over and over is, "Your college experience will be much more than just softball." I understand this, however, I really do want to play and softball will be a huge part of my collegiate life.

No matter how much rejection, disappointment, and discouragement I've been through and will go through as I continue on the recruiting journey, I know that I will end up where I belong. Despite the rejections, the stress, and the toll on my confidence, I am only a junior and still have time. Everything will fall into place; and every second spent training, emailing, and studying will have been worth it. My story is not yet over.

FINAL THOUGHTS

It is my greatest hope that this book has not only educated you about the college selection process, but also empowered you to take control of your athletic and academic destiny. As you can now see, talent is part of the recruiting process, but marketing and perseverance are equally important (if not more so). Planning is invaluable. You, your parents, and your coaches must all be on the same page. You must find ways to communicate: even when that communication seems almost impossible.

Some final thoughts:

1. Keep educating yourself about the college recruiting process. Talk with your guidance counselors, talk with happy collegiate athletes, and consider a program like A-Game.

2. Don't be foolish about how you spend your money. You would be much better off spending money on a good travel team or a Masters Program instead of going to a million different showcases and praying that someone notices you. Those hotel bills add up! Remember, sometimes spending a few hundred dollars initially can save you thousands and thousands of dollars in the long run.

3. Be realistic about your abilities and work ethic. Don't strive for Division I when you are really a Division III athlete.

4. Network, network, network!

5. Develop your support system: the team of people who will help you through this journey. For most people, this consists of parents, coaches, teammates and consultants.

6. Have a marketing strategy.

7. Stay organized.

8. Manage your social media and presence online.

9. Never, ever give up! This process can be long and difficult, but, if you follow the advice in this book, you *will* play at the school that is right for you!!!

ABOUT THE AUTHOR

Julianne Soviero is a pitching instructor, speaker, certified personal trainer, and A-Game consultant. She has produced countless award-winning athletes and has helped those athletes transition to successful collegiate careers and earn scholarships. She has appeared in various media across the country, including Fox and Sirius. Julianne is available for private consultations and seminars/speaking engagements. For more information, please contact:

Juliannesoviero@gmail.com

631-737-0196

www.flawlessfastpitch.com

www.trueathleticpotential.com